I0814232

The MEEKNESS *and* HUMILITY *of* JESUS CHRIST

The MEEKNESS *and* HUMILITY *of* JESUS CHRIST

A Life to Be Learned

CONOR GALLAGHER

TAN Books
Gastonia, North Carolina

Cover design by Jordan Avery

ISBN: 978-1-5051-3633-3
Kindle ISBN: 978-1-5051-3760-6
ePUB ISBN: 978-1-5051-3759-0

Published in the United States by
TAN Books
PO Box 269
Gastonia, NC 28053

www.TANBooks.com

Printed in India

To Jesus Christ, meek and humble of heart, who lowered Himself that I might rise and waited in silence until I came.

Contents

Note to the Reader

My Dear Reader,

Writing a book on humility is a humbling experience. The idea for this work came from one simple passing remark from a priest friend, Father Paul Check, who said to me on the phone, "You know, Jesus said 'Learn of me' only once." That was it! My mind was set ablaze. I set out reading the Gospels through a new pair of glasses, almost like an investigator looking for the lesson of meekness and humility in the life of Christ, particularly in events that do not immediately bring these virtues to mind.

In fact, the most obvious examples of meekness and humility have been the most challenging. For instance, being born in a manger or becoming the Bread of Life—the lessons in meekness and humility are so evident that, perhaps in my own pride, I was dissatisfied until another insight came to me in prayer. Yet, events in His life less associated with meekness or humility, such as driving the money changers from the temple, came to me more naturally.

Meekness and Humility

I have written of these two distinct virtues together, as they are both perfected in every act of Christ. At times, however, one shines more brightly. They are not the same. Aquinas says that humility is seeing ourselves as God sees us. There are numerous clichés about humility, such as "humility is not thinking less of yourself but of yourself less often" or "humility is knowing the truth about yourself." Aquinas's definition is not only more accurate but, I think, more helpful in day-to-day experience.

Meekness, on the other hand, is the lesser understood virtue. Aquinas, and Aristotle before him, says it is the virtue that moderates anger according to right reason. It is more typically described as power under control. Frankly, I prefer thinking of power under control rather than anger under control. A beautiful analogy is that of a mighty horse that allows a rider to climb on his back and pull the reins this way and that. I love this analogy, for traveling this life with those we love often resembles this beast of burden.

At the beginning of this project, I suspected that humility would be easy to find in the Gospels but that meekness would be less obvious. I was wrong. In fact, I was backwards. When meditating upon the God-man through the lens of meekness, His willingness to hold back His infinite power is startling. My experience on nearly every page was that of anticipation, as if the power of the Almighty would burst forth and put an end to the human nonsense He endured. I had a palpable sense of the Divine Horse able to cast off its many constraints at any moment. There is a tension throughout His life that meditation reveals, as if the veil of humanity is about to be torn asunder to reveal divinity. Bated breath is a proper response, for one day the heavens will be opened and His glory will blind those who think they see, and the eyes of those who know they are blind will be opened.

Writing to Our Lord

Addressing a work to the Lord is tricky business, both from a spiritual and literary standpoint. The example that most people think of is Saint Augustine's *Confessions*, a work that has surely influenced me.

People often forget how common this method was. We overlook Saint Catherine's *Dialogues*, large swaths of Saint Teresa's *Interior Castle*, and portions of Saint Ignatius's *Spiritual Exercises*, which include dialogues with Christ. Recently, I have spent many hours in the works of the prolific Saint Alphonsus Liguori, about half of whose writings are directed to Our Lord (or Our Lady).

The difference, of course, is that these are the works of great saints, and I am a great sinner. Solace comes to me, however, when I recall that a student of literature once told his teacher he never wanted to copy the style of a great author such as Dickens. The professor smiled and said, "Son, go right ahead; try the style of Dickens all you want." The lesson is that we can strive to emulate the greats because we will inevitably fail. Even if there is some level of success, one will naturally become different and unique by the time anything of value appears on the page.

Writing to Our Lord is embarrassing—plain and simple. It makes the writing more intimate and makes one feel vulnerable, like praying extemporaneously in public. I'm Catholic and have always lacked the comfort in this that my evangelical brethren possess. Showing the world your words to Christ makes one feel grotesquely hypocritical. Does humility demand tearing up the manuscript? If it is truly correspondence with Our Lord, has it not been accomplished without sharing with others? Am I a rich man sounding trumpets as I toss gold into the coffer?[1] Perhaps, but I hope not.

From a literary standpoint, I felt constrained by how many different ways I could say "O Lord" or "Lord, my God." I suspect David felt the same when composing the Psalms. But such is the limit of my own mind and language, and I ask for a bit of patience from the reader.

Regarding writing style, I have been told it would be classified as poetic prose. This was not my motivation; I envisioned myself writing letters to Jesus—simple as that. If I did this, I would, perhaps like most people, use the most beautiful language I could muster without sounding silly or gaudy. Admittedly, I felt this get away from me at times. I tried to pull it back and write to Our Lord in a way He deserves: plainly and simply but with reverence and eloquence.

---

[1] See Matt. 6:1–4.

40 Chapters

How does one choose the main events in Christ's life? I settled on 40 events for no reason other than that it is a good biblical number and is neither too big nor too small. Yet, I had to leave out so many glorious events that it saddened me.

For example, I included only one parable: the Prodigal Son. How does one choose which parables to include in a book like this? I don't know. I limited myself to a few public miracles and feel sorrow for not including His giving sight to the blind or telling the paralytic to take up his mat.

More importantly, I came to a screeching halt at the crucifixion. Initially, I planned on exploring His seven last words, the resurrection, and the ascension. How can any book on Our Lord's life not include these events? Here, the answer is surely not that my quota of 40 chapters ran dry; on the contrary, numerous chapters remained once I reached the crucifixion. And yet, Our Lord screamed out at me from the Cross, "Learn of me, Conor. Learn of me." All that my soul and body could do was write, "THE END". I thank God for this personal revelation. I feel confident in saying that this painstaking effort, every morning for nine months, was intended for me to learn that the cross is Christ's pulpit on which He preached the greatest sermon on meekness and humility.

And so it was; I happily went back and added a few more reflections to reach 40.

Lessons Learned

I feel compelled to share one major lesson I learned that is far too obvious to more educated men than myself. I was continually overwhelmed by the connections between passages that, previously in my mind, were separate scenes. First, some editor long ago went through the Gospels and inserted verse and chapter breaks. I have not researched who did this, nor do I really care, but I have concluded that his work was a necessary evil. Perhaps he had an impossible task before him, but I can't help but be frustrated at many of his decisions.

Before meditating deeply on a passage, I made sure to read everything before and after it. Then, in my meditation, I was astounded at the flowing waters that were dammed up by chapter breaks. If not by chapter breaks, the way we Catholics experience the Bible is usually in small chunks read day after day. So, one day, I would like to read the Gospels without any verse or chapter breaks and am certain it will be a remarkably new experience.

To demonstrate, consider Jesus calming the storm at the end of Mark, Chapter 4, and then His exorcising a demon from the man living among the tombs in the beginning of Mark, Chapter 5. In my reflection, it became clear to me that these two events are meant to be read together, for the former displays Jesus's power over nature and the latter shows His power over the supernatural. Yet, they are rarely read together because of a chapter break.

Another example: Consider the story that closes Luke, Chapter 10. Martha is reprimanded for being busy about her preparation and for criticizing Mary who sat at Jesus's feet. We all know the story. But have we considered that in the very next verse, Luke 11:1, the Apostles ask Jesus how to pray? Surely Mary, the mother of contemplatives, is meant to be seen as the precursor to teaching us how to pray. We do not consider this because of a darn chapter break.

The real point is not my frustration with chapter breaks, but that meditating on these passages shows the seamless connection of one story with another. Consider the leper in Matthew 8:2–4, an untouchable who approaches Christ with perfect faith, knowing that Jesus can make him clean. Is it a coincidence that in the very next verse, Matthew 8:5, the Roman centurion, another "untouchable" of sorts, approaches Christ with perfect faith? I think not. Yet, I had failed to see the flow of the narrative until now. And the examples can go on and on. Another book should explore these connections rarely made.

My Method

Contemplation could never be one's method of choice, for it is beyond choice. Meditation, however, is more within your control. But remember, it is not study. Meditation is allowing the story to sink deep within you. And when one thing sinks deep, it tends to pull other things in with it.

Studying is more like connecting dots and making deductions. While meditation is not contemplation, heightened meditation (for lack of a better word) is like drifting down a river by the currents as you paddle ever so gently. I was not grabbing for things. I was being drawn, just like the woman at the well was drawn to Jesus even more than the water was drawn from the well.

Meditation takes time. This entire book was written between 5:00 a.m. and 6:30 a.m., when little kids start coming downstairs. I begin my morning with the Office of Readings. It is important to begin the day with prayer completely outside of any "work" I was doing, even if the work was prayerful in itself.

I would then read the Gospel passage next on my list of 40 as *Lectio Divina* instructs. I would be sure to read the page before and after my passage to see the context.

I would implore Our Lord—sometimes the Father, sometimes the Son, sometimes the Holy Spirit, but always intentional about who I was speaking to—asking them to speak to me through the passage. And then, I would dim the light and sit in darkness, usually with little or no thoughts coming to my mind. Nearly every time, I was certain there was nothing to be revealed to me beyond the obvious meaning on the page. A glimmer of something, however, would eventually shine. And then, like a bolt of lightning, the light would become so clear that I couldn't not see it, just as looking briefly at a flash of lightning or the sun and its fiery image becomes imprinted upon the retina. I would hold that in my mind for five minutes, ten minutes, thirty minutes, until I was bursting to get it on paper.

I would then feverishly write a rough draft in my notebook. I am convinced writing with pen and paper for a project like this is infinitely better than typing on a keyboard. Later on, I would type it and begin the editing process, trying to give the Lord the language He deserves. I was surprised, however, that the first draft that came in prayer was eighty percent complete. When one is in a deeply reverent mindset, early in the morning, with a subtle light hanging over the pages of Scripture, you might be surprised how easily the words flow. So much of our day is not like this. It was a glorious experience, one that I will continue.

A Glimpse Beyond the Veil

Regarding contemplation, I am uncertain as to whether it ever occurred or not. I will say that there were many occasions when time stopped, when I lost awareness of what was going on, that my thinking stopped but my experience enhanced. An intimacy with Our Lord was felt beyond description, even when the intimacy was in the form of a reprimand or the experience of distance, as ironic as that may sound.

And then as quickly as the experience began, it would end. I felt like one moment I was walking on water, and the next I was sinking beneath the waves with hand outstretched to Jesus. Sweat had filled my brow. My breath was labored. But worst of all was the realization that it was over. In those few seconds, I would give anything to reengage Him at that level. But like a dream that drifts away by the moment, so does that zeal, that feeling, that longing to be with Him.

Whether such rare experiences were contemplation or simply practiced meditation is not the point. Rather, if this encounter with the life of Jesus can occur in me, I am certain it can happen in anyone who opens himself up to the grace pouring forth from sacred Scripture. But time is necessary. Stillness is necessary. Silence is necessary. In other words, you must be the architect of an environment conducive to this experience. No one will build this for you. You must take ownership of your day and thus provide the Holy Spirit with the tools He needs to work His grace within you.

The Lord awaits you, dear Christian reader, in every syllable of Holy Writ. Do not delay. Meet Him there. He is waiting for you. And you will learn from Him, for He is meek and humble of heart.

Introduction

". . . learn of me, because I am meek, and humble of heart . . ."
(Matthew 11:29)

O Lord, You spoke these words not just to Your disciplines, but to me. In Your divine providence, You have been slowly revealing to me the prominence of humility and the wickedness of pride. I confess, Almighty God, how pride has eluded me for so many years. I have used my intellect to comprehend the sins of the flesh, my curiosity to decipher moral conundrums (as if they were riddles to be solved), my education to play with the ideas of ancient philosophers, and my catechesis to navigate the world of virtue and vice, as if that world is a mere labyrinth to wander. But so little attention I have given to the golden path that leads into Your Kingdom: humility.

Due to Your merciful grace, I was entrusted with being the publisher of TAN Books, a publisher of many great works proclaiming Your glory. One little book, however, redefined the way I understand everything: *Humility of Heart* by Father Cajetan Mary da Bergamo (d. 1753). This little masterpiece cast the entire Christian life in terms of humility and pride. For the first time, I saw the prevalence and permutations of my own pride, so subtle and sly. I saw how the slightest act of pride was a monstrosity against Your infinite glory; that it would be better for all the world to go up in flames and the stars to fall from the sky than for me—helpless little me—to commit the smallest venial sin of pride against You, the infinite source of meekness and humility.

O Lord, I do not know which is more present to my feeble mind: the vastness of Your being or the meagerness of my own. I comprehend neither. My pride prevents me from seeing either of us for what and who we are. And yet, I must praise You for my ignorance, for I would surely die of terror if I were to clearly see either one of us.

Ever since reading *Humility of Heart*, I have desired to better know what true humility is. Since then, You have seemingly put before me Your words in Matthew's Gospel, *learn of me . . . learn of me . . . learn of me* . . . as if calling me forth, giving me a place at Your feet, like Mary who in serenity sat at Your feet while Martha busied herself in anxiety. I hear Your calling. I feel Your pull.

I have felt the desire, if not the call, to read Your life through lens of meekness and humility. You said "learn of me" only once, and You said to do so "because I am meek and humble of heart."[2] And thus, I desire to reexamine everything in Your earthly life in meditation, hoping and

---

[2] Matt. 11:29.

praying that You will show me the lessons of meekness and humility You want me to see. It has proved arduous yet rewarding beyond measure.

Enlighten my mind, Holy Spirit, so that I may show the brilliance, the glory, the majesty of the Son's meek and humble way.

My purpose, dear Jesus, is to look at Your life in this very particular way. I want to learn of You, dear Lord. I want to learn how to be meek and humble in the face of triumph and disaster, wealth and poverty, praise and scorn, pleasure and pain. I want to learn of You. I want to learn of You in the cracks and crevasses of Your little life in Bethlehem and Egypt and Nazareth. I do not want any lesson in meekness and humility to go unlearned, though I can only grasp the smallest shred of Your virtues.

I do not have a lifetime, dear Lord, to write this little book. But I do have a lifetime—however much You give me—to live in meekness and humility. One moment of humble living may well be enough to invoke Your infinite mercy. Yet, I am unsure whether I have ever done one act of true humility in my life, for pride resides in me as much as the blood running through my veins.

Do whatever You must, Lord, to bring me to meekness and humility. Do whatever You must to help me learn of You, for You are meek and humble of heart, and I am not.

I
The Idea

Whose idea was this? Did the Father propose this to You, or You to the Father? Did the Holy Spirit think up the unthinkable?

Who has heard of a sculptor becoming his own marble, a painter becoming his own brush stroke, or a composer dissolving into a single note of his opus? To my limited mind, the idea of God assuming humanity is baffling and nonsensical.

Shall I climb into the chicken coop tonight and perch on the roosting bars next to my hens? Shall I graze with my goats in the field at dawn, or forage for pollen with my bees in their quest among the clover? Such ideas are ridiculous. And yet, the idea of the divine Son of the divine Father taking on the form of a slave[3] was not ridiculous? Or was it wonderfully ridiculous, as when I make my toddler laugh by making animal noises or pretending to feed her doll with

[3] See Phil. 2:7.

a bottle? Shall I giggle like a child when I think of You becoming man?

I offer this to You, O Lord, pondering a notion so whimsically divine it seems folly: that You, a being of eternal magnitude, would lower Yourself to our mortal coil. It's a thought so outlandish, so fantastical, that only a divine intellect could conceive it. No mere creature's imagination could leap to such heights—or rather, such depths. The ancients with their demigods—Hercules, Achilles—crafted beings part-mortal, part-divine, yet none touched the essence of true Godhood. Their gods, steeped in their celestial dramas, bore no resemblance to the God of Abraham, the singular Almighty. And thus, the notion that the One Almighty God would become fully flesh and blood was never even considered. Perhaps, O Lord, no creature could have even conceived of such an idea. Our lives are constrained by logic; Your life is larger than logic.

Could any being, even the greatest of angels arrayed in splendor before time began, have ever anticipated the Incarnation? This concept, this genuine Incarnation, surpasses the fanciful tales of mythology. It's a reality that only an infinitely humble mind could fathom—a mind supreme enough to imagine being small, pure enough to consider taking on a form that, to divine sensibility, might seem a tarnishing.

The mere idea of the Incarnation speaks of Your existence, Lord. It's beyond comprehension that the Necessary would become needy, the Absolute would embrace contingency, the great I AM would become a creature. You descended not from mythic heights, from some Mount Olympus, but from a realm entirely separate, piercing an impenetrable division between the Infinite and the finite. I am that finite, that nothing; You are that Infinite, that Everything. And yet, You traversed this gulf with the humility that would later allow human hands to nail Yours to the cross—a humility that foresaw every lash, every thorn, every indignity that my own sins would inflict upon You.

Truly, only an infinitely humble God could conceive such an idea.

II
The Clash of Angels

As tradition holds, O Lord, you made the radical idea of Your Incarnation known to the angels. Your greatest of angels of the highest choir, Lucifer the Seraphim, could not bear the thought. The Angel of Light would be called to bow down to flesh and bone, artery and vein, synapse and sinew. He who could dash across the universe by the pure power of will would be called to prostrate before He who would receive applause for learning to crawl, He who would flail His arms as He learned to walk, He who would one day tire from swinging a hammer.

Truly, O Lord, he who could sling thunder bolts better than Zeus could not bring himself to adore Him who would take pleasure in skipping stones; he who could pull the sun across the sky with less effort than Apollo refused to follow Him who would one day be pulled across the desert on an ass; he who could lift the world upon his back with greater ease than Atlas could not submit himself to Him who could be crushed beneath the weight of a beam of cypress.

Until this point, if such temporal words can be used, Lucifer was in fact the crowning achievement of creation. It was somehow made known to him, however, that not only would God do the ungodliest thing imaginable (or, perhaps, beyond imaginable) and become a sniffling, sneezing, wheezing, whining baby, but that a fourteen-year-old girl would be made His queen, the queen of all angels, of all creation, the mediatrix of all graces.

I fear getting into the mind of the devil, O Lord, but it is easy for my own prideful mind to see his point. Who does not hate having pride of place taken from him? Ah—there is that word again. Pride. I know, Lord. I see it. But I cannot help asking myself: if I were as glorious as Lucifer, would I have humbled myself before Mary of Nazareth? Would I have adored the babe in a manager? How much prominence do I give to pride of place, to status, to association, to rank and privilege? Do I treat kings and servants the same?

I must admit, it is easy to worship You who has conquered the Roman Empire, who has had great cathedrals built in Your honor, the greatest art depicting Your life, the greatest music singing Your praise, the greatest minds stretching to comprehend You, the greatest poetry surging every syllable with passion for Your sacred passion. I sit here in my comfortable chair, looking back over two thousand years of triumph. Only a dunce would fail to pay You homage, to worship You, and to follow the greatest of men in their pursuit of You.

But what if rather than Your victory I only saw Your defeat? What if rather than seeing Your cardinals in cathedrals I only saw Your rabble hiding from the Romans in hovels? What if rather than smelling incense raising the prayers of the faithful to heaven, I only smelled Your earthly stench? What if rather than hearing the soothing chant of Your holy monks I only heard Your agonizing scream, "Eli, Eli, lama sabachthani!" What if rather than gazing up at a beautiful stained-glass window depicting Your passion I stood at the foot of Your cross and were splattered with blood?

Jesus of Nazareth, I live my life in gruesome pride, proud of my allegiance to You. But I am nothing more than a spoiled heir to a magnificent fortune, proud in his inheritance, fooling himself that the gold and silver are meritorious, that they are the fruits of his labor, and that if others worked they would likewise win.

Forgive me, O Lord, for I have done nothing for my inheritance.

This brings me back to Lucifer, Your once great angel. In Your infinite humility, O Lord, You allowed this glorious being to reject You and Your dearest mother, the girl of Nazareth, the Queen of Heaven. You force no one to love You. Your meekness held no chains around the Seraphic wings, and You thus allowed him to fly away, even unto the pit of hell where Your light will never shine. But he did not just leave. He waged a fearsome war against Your kingdom. Your meekness and humility allowed a great schism, a clash of angels.

In what would become Your typical way, You chose Michael from the lowly eighth choir of angels to lead Your army. You chose the humble to cast down the mighty from his throne. By the powers of nature instilled by You, Michael the Archangel held no power over the glorious Seraphim. But with his humble receptivity of Your grace, all things were possible.

It is from the very beginning of sin in the universe that we see Your meekness and humility and we see Your grace bestowed upon the humble. It is in this clash of angels where we see the foreshadowing of all that is to come, for the story of mankind is nothing but the battle between pride and humility. And the story of my own heart, O Lord, is but the same battle—the battle between loving self and loving You.

III
The Moment Between the Verses
or
The Annunciation

(Luke 1:37–38)

In the beginning, You brought the cosmos from nothing into being. But in Nazareth's tranquility, You did nearly the opposite: You emerged from the Absolute to the contingent, from Creator to creation, from the Almighty to the fragile, from the Omnipresent to the confines of DNA, atoms, cellular walls, and a Nazarene womb.

The humility of this act, Lord, of confining Yourself within human form, is beyond my grasp. The meekness required to limit Your infinite strength to vulnerability, to muscle, tendon, and sinew, is incomprehensible.

Yet, there's a humility even deeper in Your Incarnation. In the quiet of Nazareth, an act of humility took place that delved into the depths of Your divine meekness, surpassing all other actions on earth. This humility—I contend, dear Lord—outstrips even the willingness to be scourged, crowned with thorns, and crucified.

The humility I speak of is in making the Incarnation dependent upon the humility of a little girl. Divine humility sought permission of human humility. Truly, the humblest act imaginable, the incarnation, was placed at the feet of Mary, which in itself is even more humble than the incarnation itself. It's as if you said, "I will not do the humblest act unless you permit me."

At the Annunciation, Gabriel proclaimed a future still dependent on Mary's answer: "Behold, thou shalt conceive in thy womb."[4] It was yet to happen because Mary had not yet given her *fiat*, had not yet accepted Your humility.

And so, seeking understanding to love and serve better, she asked, "How shall this be done, because I know not man?"[5] Gabriel detailed the coming events, still contingent on her agreement: "The Holy Ghost shall come upon thee, and the power of the most High shall overshadow thee . . ."[6]

Is the moment between those two verses (Luke 1:37 and 38) the most crucial in all of Scripture? Your plan to redeem mankind was poised, contingent on one humble reply. Between these versified moments of scripture, the salvation of all mankind hung in the balance. I imagine heaven itself

---

4 Luke 1:31.

5 Luke 1:34.

6 Luke 1:35 –37.

may have paused, legions of angels from all choirs gathering, absorbed by the events in a small house in Nazareth, their tasks momentarily forgotten.

I wonder, did angels of the ninth choir forget their duties in order to focus on the soon-to-be Virgin Mother? I chuckle at the thought of what the world would look like if guardian angels lost their train of thought for just a moment. Did a stone mason in Rome clumsily fall off his ladder? Did some Egyptian housemaid uncharacteristically stick her finger with a needle? How many carpenters, perhaps even Joseph, slammed their thumbs with a hammer?

You have assigned not just guardian angels but Archangels to great dignitaries in both Church and civil roles. Did Herod stub his toe in front of his entourage? Did the high priest trip on his elegant vestments? Did Caesar choke on a grape?

I know, O Lord, that You assigned the fifth choir of angels, the Virtues, to govern the natural order of the universe. But did gravity cease for just a second? Did the planets lose their orbit around the sun and have to be put back on track? And did any child think he had Herculean powers as he jumped over a flowing stream because gravity ceased for just a moment? How many Germanic arrows went just above the bullseye? How many Mongols came off horseback? How many infuriated Egyptian painters could have sworn the pigments floated upward on their tomb wall? While weaving a basket for her family, did a mother in Cana sense a cosmic change? How many Greek playwrights shook their quills? And did You, O Lord, chuckle at all this and say, "It is good"?

If even the holy angels paused, what confusion must have gripped the demons, sensing the impending, transformative "yes."

Whatever the heavenly and hellish powers did at this moment, I am quite certain that sinful man's business carried on as usual, oblivious to the monumental moment that would forever change all of creation.

Your glory, the fulfillment of salvation, waited at the humble feet of a Jewish maiden. Her acceptance is the very proof of every Marian consecration and devotion, every uttered Hail Mary ever said by the greatest saints and sinners. In this divine act of humility, the Holy Trinity entrusted the plan of salvation to the Virgin's willingness.

You not only took the form of a slave but enslaved Your incarnate plan to the free will of a humble girl.

The Annunciation proclaimed not only the Incarnation but also the potential held in Mary's consent. Above all, it brought to light the profoundest depth of divine humility—a humility that sought the permission of human humility.

Then, the most humble act in history unfolded with Mary's words: "Be it done to me according to thy word."[7]

---

7 Luke 1:38.

IV
Stirring *or* The Visitation

(Luke 1:39–56)

It seems, Lord, that You orchestrated an entire scene of humility. This moment in Your earthly life, surrounded by all forms of humble expression, I suspect might have been among Your most cherished—Your divine intellect fully aware within Your mother's womb.

Your mother visited Elizabeth not only to share the miraculous conception but to witness Elizabeth's own marvel. Mystics tell us, Lord, that Mary served her cousin as a handmaid, despite Elizabeth's desire to serve her. But just as You allowed John to let water splash over Your divine head and baptize You years later, Your humility is first revealed in this moment, through Your mother, showing how holiness blossoms from lowliness.

Your humility, Lord, is evident—if we observe with the right spirit, for You are meek and humble of heart.

You, our sovereign, did the unexpected by entering our realm. And Your herald? John, the ascetic in the wilderness, a wild man of the desert, clad in camel's hair, dining on locusts.

We humans prefer accolades from the notable. Men of importance are introduced by their peers. You could have chosen any leader to announce Your coming. Instead, in perfect alignment with Your ways, You chose an outcast, a man deemed mad, dismissed by both secular and religious authorities. All those who followed the Baptist were considered a rabble of rejects, those that would soon become Your very own rabble.

In those earliest days on earth, You disclosed Yourself to John while he rested in the waters of his mother's womb. "And it came to pass, that when Elizabeth heard the salutation of Mary, the infant leaped in her womb."[8] Tradition holds that upon hearing Your mother's voice, the Baptist was baptized by Your mere presence, cleansed of Adam's sin, ready to grow in his own sanctity and prepare Your way.

"And Elizabeth was filled with the Holy Ghost: And she cried out in a loud voice, and said: Blessed art thou among women, and blessed is the fruit of thy womb. And whence is this to me, that the mother of my Lord should come to me?"[9] Elizabeth felt unworthy to receive her young cousin

---

8 Luke 1:41.

9 Luke 1:41–43.

Mary into her home. She, the older, wiser, wealthier, felt unworthy. Perhaps it was for this humility that You gave her infused knowledge of Your presence. Scripture does not say she knew Mary was with child. I assume she did not know. But Your hidden presence was all that she needed, like a saint who can sense the difference in the Holy Eucharist and an unconsecrated wafer.

If I embodied Elizabeth's humility, would the substance of things unseen become clear, or would appearances continue to guide my judgment? Would the sacred Presence be tangible beyond mere sensory perception? Would worldly beauty hold sway? Would the downcast, the lowly, the ugly, broken, infected, rejected still look so to me? Could I discern the saintly amidst their filth? Would the strong look weak and the weak look strong? How much laughter, O Lord, would sound vicious and vile? How much prudence and planning and preparation would betray me as lacking faith? How much of this kingdom of man would look and sound and feel the same?

Lord, if truly humble, I'd sense Your proximity and, in my unworthiness, plead for Your departure. But then, humility would reclaim me, compelling me to embrace Your grace, however daunting. We think we yearn for Your visage. Yet in this life, such a sight is too profound. Purify me, Lord, that I may be ready for such an encounter. Cast me into the fire of refinement, O Lord and God! Do not call me forth until I am what You desire me to be.

Mary's Magnificat, that anthem of humility, elucidates the Blessed Trinity's regard for the humble of heart, revealing that divine mercy extends to those who revere You. It speaks of scattering the proud and casting down the mighty from their thrones and lifting the lowly. You just fill the pages of Holy Scripture with humility between every letter. It spills off the pages like a mighty waterfall into the hearts of those who receive it. The promise You give to the humble is grander than all the treasures of Solomon's mines.

But when, O Lord, will You fulfill this promise? This world still seems to be controlled by the mighty on their thrones—the thrones of political power, of media influence, of the captains of industry that censor every aspect of earthly life. And yet, Rome did fall. The Chair of Peter remains while the throne of Caesar has crumbled. Christianity has spread to the four corners of the world. Your name has been spread to every nation. Still, I look around and see Sodom. I see Gomorrah. I see the world as post-Christian—not as Christian. The vicious heralds of darkness are covered in fame and glory and spotlights. Will the humble be exalted in this life? It seems not. "For my thoughts are not your thoughts: nor your ways my ways, saith the Lord."[10] And the fact that the work of Your enemies affects me greater than the triumph of Your holy name proves that I still look at life with mortal eyes.

Mary's hymn foresees a different outcome, with an eternal perspective on honor and exaltation. She sees this life as

[10] Is. 55:8.

a fleeting moment. When she thinks of exalted, she thinks eternally.

We, the proud, clamor for recognition now, not later. We long for the Kingdom to manifest in our time, for our tears to cease, for Calvary to be no more, for our earthly pilgrimage to end in victory, basking in our reward even for battles not fully fought.

In the visitation, we witness how humility fuels the endurance needed to face a lifetime of trials, which began then for Your mother and cousin, and continues in all who welcome You, hidden in the Eucharist.

Will my stomach, my heart, my confidence, and all my thoughts and passions trapped within this body stir at the first sign of Your presence? Will humility carry me through the long suffering ahead, or will my pride demand otherwise?

V
The Bread of Life
or
The Nativity

(Luke 2:1–20; Matthew 2:1–23)

The meekness and humility of Your infancy narratives are strikingly evident, O Lord. My pride yearns for something more profound, perhaps an insight others have overlooked. In other scenes of Your life, my meditation often reveals hidden truths I had never before considered. Indeed, I traversed Your entire life before returning to this beginning, unsatisfied with my understanding of Your nativity.

And yet, here it is—Your meekness and humility on full display, conspicuous to all humble eyes, revealing Your vulnerability. A naked truth, just as You entered this world. Omnipotence veiled in the tender flesh of infancy; the Word of God muffled in an infant's cry.

How was Infinity swaddled? How does the Creator have a mother?

Contemplating this paradox leaves me dizzy, much like when I attempt to grasp the concept of the Maker never being made. It is unsettling, as if I'm spiraling into an abyss. The second person of the Trinity encased in skin and bone—more implausible than an ocean captured in a child's bucket.

Your meekness allowed You to be summoned by Caesar for a census, to journey to Your birthplace on a donkey, to be turned away by innkeepers and relegated to an animal's shelter. You were warmed by the breath of beasts and adored by those who shared their earthly scent. The meekness flows from Luke's pages more mightily than the floods of Noah, for the divine power held just behind the veil is awe-inspiring.

But the metaphor upon which my mind rests, O Lord, is how the Bread of Life was laid in a feeding trough. How from all time the Bread of Life longed to be born in Bethlehem, the House of Bread. How poetic, how strategic the Almighty choreographer! An imagery so rich, so sensuous. The great poets could strive for a lifetime to devise such a metaphor but fail in the end. The beauty of your life is beyond the pale of human art.

Your first innocent cry still echoes throughout the world: "I am the bread of life."[11] All my paths, O Lord, lead back to the manger.

---

[11] John 6:35.

VI
The Passion Begun
or
The Presentation

(Luke 2:21–40)

The King of Kings, O Lord, submits to His own decree. Every leader struggles with this, for no one expects him to follow the rules governing the common man. But You, the Law itself, humbly abide by its every character and curve.

Your mother and foster father perform the sacred pilgrimage to Jerusalem to present You in the Temple. As the law prescribes for man of humble means, Joseph buys two turtledoves as an offering to Your heavenly Father. But it was not the avian blood Your Father desired. Here, in this temple of His chosen people, the Father called for the ransom of humanity: blood of the spotless Lamb.

As the innocent Isaac lay willingly beneath Abraham's blade, You laid meekly beneath the priest's. Whereas an angel of God spared Isaac's blood, no angel did for You.

Jesus, in the theater of my mind, I see legions of angels awaiting the command to stay the priest's hand. Perhaps memories of Isaac stirred in their minds. Was the Father's plan revealed to them? Or was the angelic mind amiss in confusion?

And then the knife came down, slicing the flesh embodied by the Divine. The most beautiful incarnation was cut, mauled. As the flesh was severed from the body, some part of You, Lord, was severed from the Father.

The Passion was set into motion, the Sacrifice that would save mankind continued, not merely with drawn blood, but because the foreshadowing had now become visible.

Unlike Isaac, You were not spared. No. The oblation began. As Simeon told Your mother that swords would pierce her heart, countless more afflictions would lacerate You: the slaughter of the innocents, the death of Joseph, 40 days in the desert, the demise of Lazarus that wrought Your tears, the hypocrisy of Your priests, the sadness of the rich young man, Judas's betrayal, the Agony in the Garden, Peter's denial, the thorns, the flagellum, the Via Dolorosa, the crucifixion, the utter forsaking.

Your Passion was well underway.

This foreshadowing, now radiating from the pages of Scripture, reveals another layer of meekness for constant meditation. The circumcision, the spill of the Lamb's blood, was sufficient for mankind's redemption. One drop of Your sinless blood was so rich in value that it could pay the wage of sin. In contemplating this sacred fluid, more valuable than the luster of gold, one might receive the Eucharist with heightened reverence. Forgive my oversight, Lord, for trivializing its great worth.

This one drop of blood was enough for our redemption, but it was not enough for Your love. Your meekness was so great that You not only endured the knife of a sinful man but meekly endured a Passion that would take nearly every drop of blood You possessed.

Enough for me was not enough for You.

Your meekness and humility had to give it all. Often, dear Jesus, I feel I have spent enough time with my kids or said enough prayers to meet my quota or given enough alms to soothe my guilt. One drop of blood is always enough from me. My pride rears up and says, "It is enough!" I feel I have nothing left to give, though I have hardly begun.

I beg You, Lord, let Your tremendous love displayed in the Presentation provide for me the example of giving selflessly. Enlighten my mind in times of suffering, when my physical or emotional blood is spilt, so that I see "enough" as never enough. Enable me, Lord, to embark on a life of sacrifice as You did on this day in the temple. Give me the grace to begin my passion, whatever that may be.

VII
The First Sword *or* The Slaughter of the Innocents

(Matthew 2:13–23)

"It was just a dream," I can almost hear Your virginal-father's murmur in the stillness of night. Yet this dream echoed a familiar angelic encounter, stilling his nerves about Mary. But to flee now, under cover of darkness? What words passed between Your parents?

"Mary. Mary. Wake up."

Could Mary have whispered, "Might it have been a dream?" Doubt is no sin. To wonder, to search for the sense of it all is human. Even she, unblemished by sin, sought clarity from Gabriel.

It was humble obedience that led them into the uncertain night, wordlessly disappearing. No beast could have borne their silent burden.

The angel warned of Herod's bloodlust. He knew You, a harmless child, would grow into a dangerous man. He was right. You would take his title not as a crown but as a bitter epithet above the cross. Your prophecy threatened his reign. You were the promise. He was not.

I see Mary and Joseph, bearing heavy hearts for those mothers and fathers about to face the unthinkable. The imagined blade that would claim the innocent slashed through Mary's mind. She squeezed You tightly and wept. Joseph walked faster and faster. He would weep later.

Just hours ago Mary cradled another's newborn girl among her neighbors in Bethlehem, whispering those gentle, soothing sounds only a woman can make to a baby in her arms.

The image of the blade returns, that mother's child she held now dead among the other sweet innocents. Mary moaned. Joseph panted.

The first sword had pierced Your mother's heart.

You, with infinite love for the little girl about to be slaughtered, wanted to bring heaven's wrath upon Herod and his men. Yet Your humble submission to the Divine plan kept Your sword sheathed when the soldier unsheathed his. Was it necessary to let this happen? I couldn't know. But You chose to let this drama unfold.

Perhaps in some mysterious way, Lord, in some inconceivable way I cannot fathom, You asked, "Father, can this cup pass from these children? Must they sip the bitter drink of martyrdom? Must the mothers and fathers and older brothers and sisters have this chalice poured down their throats? Is there another way, Father?"

The answer came in the silence, as You lie swaddled in Mary's arms, swaying with the donkey's rhythm. The forsaking began the moment Your blood was spilt in the temple, and it continued now. You were asked to give more than blood this time. You were asked to give Your own meekness, to restrain Your almighty arm from saving these little ones, the innocent, those that You called Your disciples to be like.

You could hear Joseph's anxiety each time he drew another exhausted breath. Mary wept for the mothers. You obeyed your Father, allowing sinful man to slaughter the innocent.

VIII
Your Father's Business *or* The Finding in the Temple

(Luke 2:41–52)

"Music is the space between the notes." And I can hear the music of Your hidden years, O Lord, echoing forth from the silence of Scripture. Questions about Your childhood, Your young adulthood, inundate my thoughts. Should my imagination soar, or should I remain anchored to the text? In prayerful reflection, I seek You in Scripture's quiet, yearning for the meekness to temper my imagination, holding it back as one reins in an eager horse, allowing it to trot but not to gallop.

My mind races back to Jerusalem, retracing Mary and Joseph's frantic steps. "Where is Jesus? Have You seen Him?" The anxiety of this sinless mother must have been acute, for a mother's anxiety is no sin at all. Memories of Herod's search, of that frightful night, and the piercing cries of bereft mothers, surely cascaded through her mind as she searched, day and night. "Mary, try to rest, if only for a moment," Joseph might have urged.

"That, Joseph, is impossible," she may have said, even as Gabriel's promise echoed in her heart. "For with God nothing shall be impossible." If the woman ever doubted anything, it could have been whether divine grace was strong enough to put her to sleep at such a moment. All night, as Joseph likely found respite in slumber, knowing that You were nearly a young man and no longer a mere child, Mary's heart was pierced anew.

What does Scripture reveal about You, Lord, as a child wandering about the city and doing Your Father's business in the Temple? Almost nothing. It tells us You "remained," suggesting purpose, not that You were merely lost. I cannot help but to wonder at Your purpose here. Amid the caravan's chaos, You might have simply drifted to a different part of the city, watching Your people fade into the horizon.

And there You were, on the cusp of manhood, with Jerusalem's grandeur unfurling before You. The streets teemed with diversity—every race, class, and creed. I imagine You thinking, "I must be about my Father's business." And Your Father's business wasn't solely within the Temple's walls. As an adult, You ministered in the streets. Did You feel a similar pull at twelve, confronted with the city's poverty? Did You share bread with a begging child, restraining the impulse to do more? Or did You do more? Did that child's family, perhaps several families, find unexpected abundance that night? Did You chuckle at Your first multiplication?

The city beckoned. It's hard to believe You spent all day in the Temple. Perhaps the adult Jesus would have, like Simeon or Anna, but a twelve-year-old? I wager, Jesus, that as Mary wept, You navigated Jerusalem's alleys, encountering the human mosaic: entertainers, merry laughter, seductive women of the street, bullying soldiers, Pharisees chastising beggars, and the desolation of the hungry and crippled.

Wandering, You might have stumbled upon the Pool of Bethesda. Around it, the desperate gathered, hoping for healing. One young man, immobilized on a mat, yearned to reach the stirring waters, stepped over by passersby. Dropping his gaze in despair, he then looked up to find You observing him. His face would be forever etched in Your memory. And You would look for him again, years later.

"His parents must have been great sinners," a young voice said behind You.

Forgive the audacity of my imagination, Lord. Perhaps I push the bounds of meekness as a writer. But could there be a sliver of truth within? Could the silence on those three days suggest a pivotal moment that shaped Your later ministry? After all, everything in Scripture is interconnected, as another interlude of three days will change the world forever. Your holy word is a feast for the storyteller. Foreshadowing abounds on countless levels, symbolism drips off every verse. The double meanings are multiplied the more You reveal Your heart. The metaphors are a gold mine. The plot twists are riveting. So, I can't help but wonder: how much of Your adult life was seeded in those three days?

For Mary and Joseph, those days were a tomb, and finding You among the scholars was akin to a resurrection. But for You? Were they the first days of Your ministry, cut short by parental wisdom? Was it the grandest of false starts, halted by a word from Mary and Joseph? "Your time has not yet come." And Your humility took this so deeply, that You waited for Your mother to call You forth at Cana.

I may not be certain, Lord, yet I believe some of the richest harmonies of Your life resonate in the silent interludes of Scripture. Among these quiet moments, my imaginings see Your encounter with the much younger paralytic, interrupted by this childlike voice behind You, tinged with a precocious pride and self-righteousness. The voice revealed a pharisaical arrogance not inherently found in one so young, but taught, instilled by those versed in religious pretense.

"His parents must have been great sinners."

This remark, brimming with judgement, must have struck You deeply, piercing You like a lance. A scowl shadowed Your face. You turned to find a boy posturing as though mature beyond his years. No words exchanged, but Your gaze alone unsettled him. He hesitated, longing to escape the discomfort but reluctant to appear childish.

"Saul! Saul!" a distant voice called, offering him a reprieve. He took off, but glanced back at You as he fled, fearing he could turn into a pillar of salt.

And You, Lord, did a hint of amusement glisten in Your eyes?

Making Your way to the temple, its splendor must have inspired awe. You might have paused, alone in thought, until a kind scholar inquired about Your solitude. Perhaps the boy's arrogance got you wondering about the inheritance of sin. And the piercing insight of Your questions garnered a crowd of wisemen, reminiscent of how Your nativity garnered another group of wisemen in Bethlehem.

Then, Your parents burst in. Mary, with a mother's relief, showered You with hugs and kisses, much to the amusement of the scholars, much to Your embarrassment. You wiped her kiss off. You lost Your audience.

"Did You not know I would be about my Father's business?"[12]

This exchange hints at the divine dance between Your unfolding mission and the prudent protection by Your earthly guardians, a delicate balance I am sure Mary and Joseph felt keenly. You would have days on the road to Nazareth to discuss it.

You returned home, changed in some unspoken way—a testament to humility, mastering patience. Though You are the incarnate Word, You seemed to learn something: to bridle Your power, postponing Your ministry until the appointed time was revealed. And it would be revealed by the woman who likely made it clear during that homeward journey that Your time had not yet begun.

---

12 Luke 2:49.

Lord, revealing the human aspect of Your youth and the delicate maternal side of Mary is an act of profound humility. Thank You. I need this side of Your life. The more I relate to Your humanity, Lord Jesus, the more I adore Your divinity.

IX
The King of Rabble
or
Behold, the Lamb of God

(John 1:23–36; Matthew 3:1–17)

You had a myriad of options for a herald. Imagine if King Herod himself had been chosen, or the high priest, or even a renowned scholar. You might have unveiled Your divinity to Caesar and, with a mere act of Your will, had him lay his crown upon Your holy head and nations prostrate before You.

In my limited understanding, swayed by worldly logic, sometimes I wish You had. To the human mind, it defies reason to herald the world's greatest news through an outcast, a crazy man, a wild voice crying out in the wilderness.

Yet many of Your prophets were unconventional, Lord, so it's no surprise that the greatest among them, John the Baptist, was more than just unconventional. His attire of camel hair, his diet of locusts and wild honey—these are not the futures we dream of for our children. But this man's asceticism, his fervent denunciations of Herod, his biting rebukes of the Pharisees and Sadducees, were cherished by You. You saw in this man something no one else could see and thus bestowed upon him the greatest praise possible. "Among those born of women there has not risen one greater than John the Baptist."[13]

It was a deliberate act of restraint, a humbling choice, to be heralded by an outcast. This ensured You would be viewed with suspicion from the beginning. John, ostracized and ridiculed by the ranks of power, prepared a backdrop against which You would step forth, bearing the weight of their scorn from the outset. Why begin Your mission this way, Lord? Did You wish for a more challenging path by choosing a radical to announce Your arrival? You permitted a radical to baptize You, making You a radical in the eyes of both Your adversaries and Your puzzled followers. Were You not greater than John? Did Your soul need purification?

You seem, Lord, to have little problem with sowing seeds of confusion. Two millennia later people remain perplexed by Your baptism, just as—I assume—those first witnesses were. Did You do this to identify with humanity, to foreshadow Your death and resurrection, to launch Your ministry?

---

13 Matt. 11:11.

Whatever Your reasons were, my God, Your humility to step into the water with John was a willingness to embrace the identity of an outcast, a radical, an eccentric.

Jesus of Nazareth, King of Rabble.

And then there's me, hyperaware of others' perceptions. Always concerned about how I sound or come across, finely tuned more for reputation or agenda than for unwavering truth or pure charity.

How often my ulterior motives spin intricate webs of calculated expression and strategic movement. O, how often I find myself entangled therein! All the while a simple, forthright expression of truth and kindness would be the balm that sooths my nerves and the drink that refreshes my soul.

Your humility, Lord, bypassed the entrapments of vanity. How I long for this serenity! Perhaps it was this very detachment that granted You peace: Your mind free from schemes for influence, Your heart filled with love for neighbor and a forgiveness for adversaries.

Your relationship with this reject, this outcast, this mad man of the desert unmistakably shows Your humility. And John's declaration, echoed in all four Gospels, that he was unworthy even to untie Your sandals, mirrors Your humility with poetic grace.

From these accounts, I sense You call me to focus solely on truth and love, fostering a healthy disregard for public opinion. I am not summoned to the austerity of the desert, nor to subsist on locusts and wild honey, yet my spirit should be as unattached as John's was. Yet, instead of letting ego indulge in delicacies, I should sustain it on the humble fare of truth and charity. If charity is my honey, must I suffer the stings of life's swarm to taste its sweetness? Perhaps so. Perhaps that is the very path to genuine humility.

X

Pleasure
or
The First Temptation in the Desert

(Matthew 4:1–11; Mark 1:12–13; Luke 4:1–13)

Immediately, Jesus Christ, exemplar of humility, You enlighten my path with the opening words of this profound episode of Your life. "Then Jesus was led by the Spirit."[14]

In seeking to emulate Your humility as You have beckoned, and possessing a mere fraction of the virtues I chase, I could dwell upon this singular verse for hours, days, or weeks.

Did You, O Lord, in Your human nature, have a singular intent with the Father and Holy Spirit, or were You led to a place not of Your choosing? On day one did You fear what was coming? On day twenty ravaged with hunger did you

---

14 Matt. 4:1.

say, "It is enough"? On day thirty, with Your throat so dry that sand looked soothing, did You beg Your Abba to let this chalice be replaced with a cup of water?

As the Son of Man, did You negotiate with Him as Moses did long before? Did You wrestle with divinity as Jacob had? The divine enigma of Your being, wrapped in human flesh, eludes me; contemplating it sends a tremor through me, a minor shock.

"My mind rebels," I whisper to myself, craving logic, reason, tangible facts. "Who authored You, O God?" It is like peering into an infinity mirror, where endless reflections spiral into an infinite regression. Like a child between these two mirrors, amusement swiftly turns to unease. Today, that feeling resurfaces when I ponder You being "led by the Spirit," and more so, Lord, when I meditate on the Spirit ushering You into the wilderness to endure temptation.

Did Your vivid memories of these temptations cause You to add "lead us not into temptation" into the prayer You taught us? This seems logical to a man, but You, O Lord, while never illogical, are beyond logic. The mysterious depths of Your hypostatic union are beyond my grasp, as I scarcely grasp the inner workings of those finite beings closest to me. Looking at Your life, Lord, can feel like peering out into space, knowing the distance that lies before me can barely be put into a metaphor.

In Your boundless humility, You willingly followed the Spirit deep into the barren desert. Although united with Your Father in intimacy, You yearned for more, if such a thing were possible. And so, like the prophets before, You fasted, eschewing every earthly pleasure to open Yourself to the Divine Word. You knew that an even greater intimacy with Your Father lay beyond the forty days of forsaking. How can this be, O Lord? How can a perfect relationship be further perfected?

I envision You, Lord, after those forty days: gaunt, each step an exertion against drained muscles, skin parched as the sand, lips cracked. Did You ration water to mere survival? Was Your throat as raw as I imagine? Did the desert sun cause Your head to throb with pain? Did You wonder at John's endurance in such harshness? Did You foresee St. Antony of the Desert and admire his strength?

The Spirit led You into the desert, but where is it leading me? Do I recognize my own deserts? Can I hear the call to be a trustful servant amid life's noise? The Church beckons toward gentle purifications, yet I struggle with even the simplest mortifications. The excuses to abandon the desert are countless. The sole reason to remain is the same that kept You there—humility.

Was this agony in the desert meant to prepare You for the Agony in the Garden? What divine insights, if any, graced Your mind, or were You stripped of comfort and revelation alike?

When the moment came, when You were perhaps at Your weakest, the Evil One saw fit to tempt You. He offered what any man might crave—a simple loaf of bread, a loaf of pleasure to satiate the body's cravings. Lead us not into temptation, Lord, for pleasure is the Devil's gambit. Our response must echo Yours. For we chase after varied forms of "bread"—wealth, desire, esteem—allowing pride to drive us to seek fulfillment in the transient, the passing, that which can grow stale and moldy and rancid.

At our weakest, the reminder floods the mind: we have the power to comfort ourselves at any moment! The Son of God might be able to turn stones to bread, but I can simply walk into my pantry. Such power we hold, and yet, to restrain it is to truly embrace humility. I can almost hear Your parched voice, reaffirming Scripture's truth: "Man shall not live on bread alone, but on every word that comes from the mouth of God."[15]

May these words spoken from Your lips resonate within me whenever I seek worldly solace over divine sustenance. May I only find comfort in the Word of God, and the Word of God alone.

15 Matt. 4:4.

XI
Presumption *or* The Second Temptation in the Desert

(Matthew 4:5–7; Luke 4:9–13)

Then, O Lord, You were taken to the temple's pinnacle. Scholars debate which pinnacle this was. It may have been the peak. Or it may have been over the entrance so all could see You as they entered. In either case, You could have put on a grand spectacle with a host of angels rushing to Your rescue as an angel saved Isaac from Abraham's knife.

The evil one was not only tempting You to spectacle, but to presumption. In this moment, a chill runs through me, my conscience is rattled, my hand trembles. Every day, presumption beckons me to cavalier reliance on Your Father's mercy. Michelangelo depicted my soul, O Lord, when he frescoed the Sistine Chapel with Adam's limp and languid hand. I sit here, bathing in pools of grace, awaiting Your mercy to reach for me. Raised in the Church, surrounded with love, inspired by the traditions, sacraments at my daily disposal. Mercy has swaddled me like a baby. I have been nourished on compassion.

I have thrown myself down from the pinnacle of my life in myriad ways, always saved by one form of Your mercy or another. And so, Lucifer's whisper "throw yourself down" again and again. His words to You resonate with unnerving familiarity. It plays upon my greatest vulnerability: the presumption of Your boundless mercy. I am spoiled, O Lord. I am spoiled.

I feel a great chasm in my soul between Your justice and mercy. How can these two infinite virtues coexist? Yet I know there is no division within You. And here, O Lord, is the great question that brings anguish to my heart: is it easy or hard to get to heaven?

Scripture paints a daunting path: it is harder for a rich man to enter the Kingdom of Heaven than for a camel to pass through a needle's eye;[16] broad is the path to perdition, and narrow is the gate to life.[17] I know, Lord, I know. Yet, Your parables speak of a repentant sinner's warm embrace.

I am a father and would willingly be the prodigal father, standing on the front steps, gazing into the horizon, hoping for the return of my beloved son. I will clothe him with the finest robe, put rings on his fingers, slaughter the fatted

---

16 See Matt. 19:24.

17 See Matt. 7:13.

calf, and call all my loved ones to celebrate the return of my dearest boy. Truly, my heart is eager to pardon my child at the faintest sign of remorse. He need not be sorry for his sins to obtain my forgiveness; he must only be sorry that he is not sorry. I gladly reach into that crack of repentance and throw it open wide so that my mercy can flow through with mighty force.

If my flawed fatherhood mirrors Your perfect paternity in other ways, would You not forgive me more readily than I would forgive my son? Would You, my God, as my Prodigal Father who lavishly bestows mercy, not rush to meet me, clothe me in grace, and celebrate my return more joyously than I could for my own child?

Yet, how do I reconcile this parable, showcasing Your infinite mercy with Your odious warnings of a narrow path? In my limited mind, the chasm between these concepts is wider than the most colossal canyons. I cannot see the bottom. I cannot see across. An endless void seems to fill the gap.

Will Your infinite meekness not spare me the just sentence I deserve? Will Your boundless humility look for any excuse to welcome me home?

The tempter's hiss reaches my ear: "Cast yourself down. Doesn't Your divine Father cherish You enough to dispatch legions of angels for Your rescue?" Such whispers coax me toward presumption, luring me into a false security.

Presumption, the very trial You confronted amidst the desolation of the wilderness, now confronts me amidst the abundance of grace. "To whom much is given, much is required." How these words strike terror in my soul!

Truly, O Lord, there is a great burden of abundance, namely presumption, a sin so often forgotten, barring my journey to the depths of love and the peaks of sanctity. Is presumption not the most covert adversary of humility? I do not tally my virtues, Lord God; such is not how pride attacks my soul. Yet, the assumption of Your grace is my daily ledge from which I leap, trusting for salvation even as I plunge.

XII

Pragmatism *or* The Third Temptation in the Desert

(Matthew 4:8–11; Luke 4:5–8)

The third temptation You faced, O Lord, was the lure of dominion: to bow before Satan for the prize of the world. Scripture recounts he showed You the kingdoms of the world. The tempter granted You a mystical experience as never enjoyed by any other man. Did You see kingdoms of every land and of every age, past and future? Did You see not only kingdoms of royalty but of my own kingdom of comfort?

The devil whispered his offer in Your ear as You gazed upon the grandeur of every kingdom of man to ever stand, that would ever stand: "To You, I will give all this authority and their glory; for it has been delivered to me, and I give it to whom I will."[18] Indeed, Satan has been dubbed "the ruler of this world"[19] and "the god of this world."[20] It is no stretch to believe that throughout history, many have indeed prostrated themselves, literally or metaphorically, before the Evil One to ascend the heights of their industry. They have bartered their integrity at the crossroads for fleeting glories and worldly dominions. The rapid rise of certain artists with questionable talents, the inexplicable viral nature of mediocre art, or the instant fame or fortunes of individuals seemingly overnight—might these not be bargains struck at great cost?

Yet, Lord, You walked a different path. Despite the staggering truth that after millennia, Your Gospel has yet to reach every soul, despite the decline of reverence and adherence to the teachings You entrusted to Your Church, You chose not to harness the seductive power of the tempter. In Your infinite humility, You resisted the practicality of compromising even a sliver of truth for the sake of expedient success. The end did not justify the means for You, as it all too often does for me.

You came into this world to bring a message. You could have bent Your knee ever so slightly, and Caesar would have prostrated before You. The smallest concession of Your will was all that was needed, and Your message could have been

---

18 Luke 4:6.

19 John 12:31.

20 2 Cor. 4:4.

spread to the four corners of the Earth. But making the slightest concession, You never even considered.

How often, Lord, do I find myself weighing the advantages of the slightest concession. I entangle myself in gray areas of moral decisions: shall I boycott platforms that showcase blasphemous content? Shall I only invest ethically, compromising potential gains? How proximate can my association with evil be? Shall I engage in idle speak about that person in the name of getting advice from another? If one is moralistic, one sees moral dilemma everywhere.

In the face of the world's pragmatism, Your humility was unyielding, trusting in the eternal fruits of righteousness rather than the immediate harvest of compromise. Pragmatism may offer quick fixes, but faith calls us to a higher standard. Thus, we must willingly enter our deserts of prayer and fasting. Only then will the divine path be illuminated amidst the worldly dazzle that seeks to blind us.

It is in Your humility, Lord, that the true course of life is discerned. It is through a body broken in the desert, a spirit laid bare, that the soul finds clarity. Lead me into my desert, Lord Jesus; ready or not, grace me with the purity needed to walk the path You set before me.

And when the temptations have passed, may a company of ministering angels bring me solace as they did You, that I may be fortified in suffering and steadfast in my journey toward holiness.

XIII
Two Gazes
or
The Wedding Feast at Cana

(John 2:1–11)

Gracious Lord, my heart swells with gratitude for this depiction of tender closeness shared between You and Your blessed Mother. It captures such an earthly moment, exalted by the overlay of Your divine presence—a microcosm reflecting the grand mystery of Your Incarnation. Sharing this with us beckons contemplation; an invitation to cherish those gentle exchanges with Mary, as she summons us to heed our own calling.

It is here, at the wedding feast, that I see the narrative arch of our mystical marriage with You, O Lord. The story of salvation begins with a marriage-like union between Adam and Eve before the Fall, a prototype of our mystical union with You. And then holy Scripture ends with another marriage, the heavenly Jerusalem drawn up to marriage with the Lamb—the Church's mystical union with You.[21]

But the arc of this narrative continues here, in the little town of Cana, with more imagery than this work can unfold. There is a bridegroom at this wedding, but You, O Lord, are the Divine Bridegroom, transforming not just water into wine, but the old covenant into the new. And Your Blessed Mother shows herself as the New Eve and Mother of the Church, bringing You forth into both Your passion as well as Your glory. Yes, the entire story of salvation can be shown as the three-part story of our mystical marriage to You, the Divine Bridegroom. Scholars of the Scriptures hear echoes of the Old Testament in the six stone jars: six representing incompleteness, yet over 180 gallons of drink symbolizing the abundance of grace to be given. Theologians rightly emphasize the moment when Your mother called You to public ministry. This strikes a chord within my soul, especially when pondering how she once restrained You—at the age of twelve in the Temple. I enjoyed imagining Your youthful explorations in Jerusalem for three days, finding all sorts of foreshadowing of Your three-year ministry, with perhaps a little too much youthful haste to begin Your destiny. Indeed, Scripture recounts that You grew in wisdom[22]—a portion of which, I surmise, sprang from the wisdom of heeding Your mother's word. Not only a supernatural prudence in the case of an immaculately conceived mother, but prudent advice for

---

21 See St. John Apoc. 19:7.

22 See Luke 2:52.

most young men as they stumble through the turbulence of maturation.

Theologians have pondered over calling Your own mother "woman." Annotations in sacred texts strive to clarify that far from a slight, it was acknowledging her as the New Eve, the woman foreordained to redress the downfall ushered by her predecessor.

That's all fine.

Yet, it is the words of a poet that seem to be the greatest of commentaries, tapping into an insight of which theologians can only dream: "the waters saw their Creator, and blushed."[23] No scholarly exposition can pierce the essence of creature meeting Creator more beautifully than this. And is the most beautiful of words the most accurate? Perhaps so when Beauty Itself is the subject. Your Incarnation infused the divine into our realm, justifying the personification of all elements in the universe. If stones could sing, they would rival Pavarotti in their chorus. If sticks could make music, they would match Mozart. And if water could sense the gaze of Your eyes, it would blush. Nothing short of masterful.

I reflect upon Your earliest disciples, who had been with You a mere three days by the time You reached Cana. You have not garnered Your disciples with tricks to impress them. This fact alone resounds with profound significance. Your initial call to them was not underscored by grandiose miracles or spectacle. Rather, it was the simple yet powerful

---

23 Richard Crashaw, *Book of Sacred Epigrams* (London, 1682), 7.

endorsement of John the Baptist that drew them near. The command "Come, follow me" was sufficient, and at Your behest, they dropped their nets. O, to envision the depth of sincerity in Your gaze that prompted such an immediate surrender! I fear no artist ever has nor ever will capture the look on Your face—or theirs.

I think, Lord Jesus, Your meekness desired to win your disciples over by natural means. You didn't want to use Your strength and glory to attract Your closest friends. Would You have preferred to win them over by Your charm and wisdom rather than miracles? And did You see Your mother's call as interrupting this plan? Sometimes one's father—or mother—has different plans than we do. I enjoy thinking of Your plans being changed, just as mine are at times. You are like me in all things but sin.

At that pivotal moment with Your disciples, Your mother's mere presence set the course of events into motion. Revisiting this passage over and over again, I see a new layer. When she said to You, "They have no wine," You did not only say, "What does this have to do with me?" but You said, "Woman, what concern is that to you and to me?"[24] This subtle addition of "to you" hints at a shared understanding of the path ahead. In Your hesitation, there was a concern for her—aware that the first irrefutable miracle would not only alter Your course but inevitably cast her into the public sphere, thus ending her simple, quiet life. And she would not even have the luxury You would have

[24] Jn 2:4 (NRSVCE).

of moving from town to town when rumblings about Your ministry stirred up problems.

Alas, the Mediatrix seemingly ignored Your aversion to the crisis. She said nothing with her words and everything with her eyes, as true women often do. A poetic dance ensued by the silent stare from her immaculate eyes into Yours. And there were two transformations that followed two gazes.

A mother's gaze into a son's eyes—eyes tinged with anxiety for the transformation from cloistered Son of Man to manifested Son of God, from son of a carpenter to Savior of the world. Your heart fluttered into submission, Your will stirred with consent. "Do whatever he tells You," she said to the servants. She turned and left. And You turned—You turned toward Your mission. You turned into the public figure. You turned toward the six jars of water. And the tranquil clarity of Your spirit deepened into a resolute crimson, foretelling Your coming Passion. Your time was now.

Then, with Your mother's certitude, You looked into the water, and it turned.

In acquiescing to her subtle but firm gaze, Your humility proved as fluid as the water in those jars, conforming to the container's shape. You conformed to Your Father's and mother's will. Like the water, You molded Yourself with complete surrender to divine providence and to the mediation of Your blessed mother.

Thus, in emulating this trust and surrender, we become like the water—freely, fluidly, willfully assuming the form divinely ordained for us. The utmost expression of meekness is to mold oneself to God's will, and in the full relinquishment of our own designs, to accept our place within the sacred present, we undergo a transformation as profound as water to wine. As long as I cling to my own plans, I remain cold, unremarkable, like ice. Yet, by surrendering to Your exemplary humility, I become as graceful as water. Only then can I too be transmuted into an offering fit for the heavenly feast.

XIV
Remembering Joseph
or
The Cleansing of Heart and Temple

(John 2:13–22; Matthew 21:12–13; Mark 11:15–17; Luke 19:45–46)

When at first glance I cannot see a particular virtue in this scene from Your life, I know that there is a hidden depth escaping my sight. This, O Lord, likely stems from my own perspectives skewing my view of Your actions—a kind of projection. Do I inadvertently ascribe my own failings to You?

Were I to drive people out or even call attention to myself in public view, claiming meekness and humility would be far from truth. Yet, in moments where You may seem to prioritize righteousness over meekness and humility, it is precisely then I must delve into the understated presence of these virtues. You, Lord, are the master of paradox, never an enigma of contradiction.

Passover is at hand. You and Your new followers, aglow from Cana's miracle, journey from Capernaum to Jerusalem. I envision them, expecting to perform the ritual sacrifice, counting coins for offerings. I see You, pausing at a vendor's booth to purchase leather cords, whittling away at the modest sums in the common purse. Were the chords twelve inches, two feet, a lengthy six feet? Did Your disciples whisper amongst themselves in confusion at Your purchase?

Upon entering the temple and proceeding with piety to the merchants' tables, I observe You selecting a secluded nook to settle into. You begin to methodically coil the cord, securing it firmly with each twist. With every intertwining, You pull the chord tighter and tighter, prayers grow more fervent alongside righteous anger welling within.

Did Your eyes keep looking up, beholding one family after another trying to make sense of the exchange rate? Did You see a wealthy man proudly purchase an ox, symbolizing his own power to push and pull others with his riches? Did you see a solitary widow, her later years marred by loneliness, parting with her scant savings to buy a lamb at an inflated price, a creature representing her own innocence and purity?

And did Your heart go out to a ragged family, wearied from their travels, the father negotiating for fair currency? Was his restrained vexation an anamnesis, recalling Joseph's very same frustration? Did the memory flood Your mind of tugging at Joseph's sleeve as a little boy, wanting to point out the flawed math used by the moneychanger? "Not now, Jesus," he would gently chide. And, mirroring Joseph's humility, the ragged family accepted the overcharge, shuffling over to the next line to acquire the offering reserved for the impoverished: a pair of doves. Confronted with the inflated cost, the father shook his head in disbelief, yet out of reverence, he complied. Their long journey gave them no other recourse.

Your gaze fell on the moneylenders and merchants, the cords tightening in Your grip, Your jaw clenched. Your disciples silenced themselves as Your eyes stopped blinking, and they saw your fixation. Memories of Joseph surged.

Now, You are angry. A yearning for vengeance for both Your earthly guardian, oppressed by systemic corruption, and Your divine Father, betrayed by the greed of His chosen people. The prophetic verses flood Your mind: "Is this house then, in which my name hath been called upon, in your eyes become a den of robbers? I have seen it, saith the Lord."[25] "I will bring them into my holy mount, and will make them joyful in my house of prayer: their holocausts, and their victims shall please me upon my altar: for my house shall be called the house of prayer, for all nations."[26]

A house of prayer. A den of robbers. Such thoughts, such prophies rushed through Your mind. It was time for mea-

---

25 Jer. 7:11.

26 Is. 56:7.

sured force to vindicate the honor of Your fathers. Perhaps the final words of Zechariah resonated with You: "the merchant shall be no more in the house of the Lord of hosts in that day."[27] That day had come. Your time had come.

You stood slowly with humility and meekness, and humbly obeyed that still, small voice harking You to action. It shocked Your followers. It lacked the spectacle of water to wine, yet it was equally profound. You "drove them all out of the temple" along with "the sheep and oxen." I envision the vendors fleeing Your scourge, some of whom may have reveled in Your own scourging thereafter. The oxen stampeded across the stone floor as crowds of pilgrims hid behind marble columns. You unleashed chaos in this sacred place.

As You confronted the money changers, they saw resoluteness in Your eyes, just as many of us will see on our judgment day. You overturned their tables, coins clashing against sacred grounds that should be reserved for reverence. In the end, You indeed brought them to their knees in Your Father's house, kneeling amidst their scattered coins, scrabbing them up as if they were sacred idols.

Yet, in the following verse, I perceive a new facet of Your meekness. Your anger subsides; Your scourge drops to the ground. You pause, collect Yourself, catch Your breath, before addressing those who sell doves. You spared them, choosing words over wrath. You did not open the cages and shoo the doves into the sky.

But why?

---

27 Zach. 14:21.

Why did you preserve this group of men and animals? You spoke to them instead. Did You speak gently? Or did Your voice thunder with celestial clarity, raising Your hand like John the Baptist yelling "Repent!"?

Perhaps, Lord, You spared these sellers and their wares, for the dove symbolizes the poverty of the masses, the sole offering the impoverished, like Your father Joseph, could afford. Should I be surprised You spared the offerings of the poor? I imagine that with profound gentleness, You proclaimed, "Take these things hence, and make not the house of my Father a house of traffic."[28]

In this You instruct us in the humility of meekness—not by expulsion, but through counsel. Yet the paramount lesson in this upheaval of merchants and moneylenders is the divine yearning for a humble and contrite heart—the only sacrifice from me for which my God yearns. The ritual of bloodshed will be eclipsed, for You are to be the final blood-victim. God will forever seek from us not the blood of beasts, but the offering of our will. His temple will become bloodless. Incense will no longer be used to cover the stench of carnage, but as a symbol of our devotion rising to heaven, just as our hearts shall soar toward the Father on the wings of those spared doves.

---

28 John 2:16.

XV
Drawing the Woman
or
The Woman at the Well

(John 4:1–42)

My Lord, my God. You're never doing just one thing. You orchestrate time with the strategy of a chess grandmaster while Your disciples and I struggle to play checkers, seeing life in one little move at a time. Oh, how many times I forget this. I see Your hand at play and in my pride think I know Your plan. I see Your tactic and think I know Your strategy.

In Your mercy, dear Jesus, You often permit a glimpse of a deeper design, Your unstated aim behind the veil of the conspicuous. When I pause to silence my heart and still my soul, You often reveal Your profound workings in my life, and more importantly, in the lives of those I love.

At times I can relate to this woman at the well, burdened with shame, withdrawn from fellowship. Fatigue sets in;

I reach my threshold. Everyone seems to demand more of me—more time, more resources, a ceaseless litany of requests. They beckon me to journey forth, to draw water, to shoulder the burden. I fulfill these duties, begrudgingly.

Yet, there You rest, quietly asking more of me, not dissimilar to how You slept in the stern of the ship amidst a raging storm.[29] "Draw water for yourself," she must have thought, just as Your disciples wished You to bail water with them. You seem to ask more of us when our duties are already manifold.

The story, however, unfolds beyond mere tasks. Your plea, "Give me to drink,"[30] is less about quenching physical thirst—akin to Your cry on the cross—than about a profound spiritual longing. In asking me to draw water, You are drawing me closer to You.

So it was with the woman at the well. A thirst so profound, one greater than You had after forty days in the desert, brought You to Jacob's well. You were parched, famished, yearning, longing for the Samaritan's soul. You led her down a path only to reveal a hidden journey beneath the surface, as You often do in my own life. Your meekness and humility are so evident after praying over this passage for days on end.

Your journey to Samaria was a humble act for the King of the Jews. You approached a people to be avoided. Salvation was outside of these lost sheep. Your disciples, likely

---

29 See Mark 4:38.

30 John 4:7.

perplexed, would have been discouraged in this backward turn Your ministry had already taken. Was their teacher such a reject that he could not even minister to the Chosen People?

Then, You find Your way to Jacob's well, which may have been the very well where Jacob fell in love with Rachel, a sacred site imbued with romantic undertones. Here You were, a single man, sitting at a place where You were surely to meet women after sending Your disciples away. She arrives at noon, in the heat of the day to avoid the other women who castigate her lifestyle. You are alone with her, man to woman.

The humility leaps from the verses. Not only were You visiting a filthy people, but You were alone with a woman deemed filthy by the filthy. What man of virtue would be caught in such compromise? You knew Your disciples would see this. And they did.

You asked her for water, which some might construe as a covert courtship. Certainly, an overly sensualized woman might misread even the purest intentions. I envision Your humility, permitting a misjudged perception. You play a strategic game far beyond the comprehension of those confined to simpler interactions. Yet, Your ultimate aim is to draw this lost soul to Yourself. You thirst for her soul while at least five men have thirsted for her flesh.

This entire scene, Lord, shows me how You make sacraments of mundane events; You baptize the natural with the sacred.

You offer her living water. She does not understand. You make a seemingly casual inquiry about her husband, easily construed as a path well-traveled by the common man, gauging her attachments. "I have no husband," she replies.

At this moment, Lord, You have drawn her in. She is Yours. Was her statement matter of fact, or was she telling an attractive man, "I am available"? I pray I do not insert the profane into the sacred texts, but I see that part of Your humble presence among us is sharing in our ways, except, of course, in sin. You know the games we play. You recognize flirting when You see it. Clearly, many beautiful women batted their eyes at You through the years. Perhaps fathers proffered their daughters to Joseph for arranged marriage, or directly to You upon his death. We have seen the wine at Cana blush, but You? If You wept and marveled, why would You not blush? My mind ablaze!

In an instant, You flip this encounter on its head. "You have had five husbands."

Can the term *blush* do justice to the crimson red that overtook her face? Did the bucket drop down the well? Did she feel she was drowning in her own history, her heart plummeting with the bucket into the depths?

A revelation occurs. A sin is laid bare. An unveiling of the true purpose of Your presence. She perceives You as a prophet.

With humility almost too profound to fathom, You reveal Yourself to this woman, an outcast among her people. You choose her as Your messenger to the Samaritans, mirroring Your choice of John the Baptist, another forsaken by society. Your disciples, observing this, may wrestle with similar thoughts of scandal, yet they exercise discretion in their silence.

As she departs as Your herald to announce the Messiah, Your meekness unfolds before Your disciples. Perhaps You let their curiosity simmer. Yet You redirect their conversation about food to the spiritual harvest before them.[31]

O Lord, this extraordinary portrait of humility and meekness cannot be captured in words. Clearly, it was contagious, and this woman willingly proclaimed You, despite her past life, as the Christ before her people.

Can I do the same as this filthy woman? Can I, despite my past, current, and future sins, be Your herald in this modern world? Can I allow my sins to drop with the bucket, deep into the well, and disappear into Your mercy? Only then will I have the fortitude and zeal to proclaim Your presence to the people of this fallen world.

---

[31] See Matt. 13:37–43.

XVI
The Strangest Commandment *or* The Sermon on the Mount

(Matthew 5:21–49)

O Lord, You have bestowed upon us a definitive guide through Your teachings—eight Beatitudes, each a path to understanding Your meekness and humility, a lesson on how we are to learn of you. But You show us here that we must not only be humble in our actions but likewise in our intentions. For just as Your Father called the Israelites to be pure and clean outwardly, You further call us to also be pure of heart and mind.

You elaborate on the essence of the Beatitudes, offering a deeper interpretation of the Ten Commandments. You challenge us to look beyond the literal act of murder, revealing that even anger toward our brother strikes at the heart of the commandment.[32] You unveil the truth that adultery begins in the heart, well before it manifests in action.[33] You urge us to confront our worst instincts with stark imagery—removing the eye or hand that leads to sin,[34] and You teach us the integrity of a simple "yes" or "no", the courage to turn the other cheek, and the generosity to offer more than what is taken from us.[35]

You have turned the world upside down with these teachings. You call us to first amend our hearts, and our actions will follow, for once we have meekness and humility imprinted on our hearts, our lives will be led by them. We take it for granted in a post-Christian world. These teachings, O Lord, perfectly culminate in two declarations that astound the mind.

First, "Love Your enemies."[36] This directive seems to contradict every instinct embedded in human nature. Natural law impels parents to teach their children to distinguish right from wrong, kindness from cruelty, but to love one's enemy? To bless those who curse us? Does this divine revelation challenge us to transcend our nature more than to abide by it?

---

32 See Matt. 5:21–22.

33 See Matt. 5:28.

34 See Matt. 5:29–30.

35 See Matt. 5:37–40.

36 Matt. 5:44.

And then, the most perplexing of Your edicts: "Be perfect, as your heavenly Father is perfect."[37] How does one grapple with a command that seems unattainable? To love an enemy, to forgive, to seek peace—these are within reach. But perfection? I know, Lord, being perfect consists in fulfilling one's nature. A perfect rock is different than a perfect stick. A perfect dog is different than a perfect cat. And so, are these counter-intuitive decrees of Yours the perfection of human nature? Or is it a transcendence of my nature?

Your great saint, Bernard of Clairvaux, would explain perfection as the mystical union of the soul with You, O Lord, the Bridegroom, so elegantly sung in the Canticle of Canticles. And Your great saints of the East, such as Maximus the Confessor, would explain perfection as *theosis*, deification, in which we are called to become God-like through participation in Your divine grace. Some argue that this calling to perfection is nothing more than a calling to eternal life in heaven.

How can we not dwell on this commandment, O Lord, without ceasing? How can we not bend our minds, scour the writings of the saints, and beg for insight from Holy Scripture, to better understand the strangest commandment? Shall I dismiss Your words as hyperbole? Shall I take You literally? Take me, Lord, into the inner chamber[38] of

---

[37] Matt. 5:48.

[38] See Cant. 2:4–6.

Your mind and heart. Show me Your secrets. I am unworthy, O Lord, but I stand knocking at Your door.[39]

In contemplating this passage, I hope a glimmer of its meaning comes to my feeble mind. It is not, I think, solely a call to heavenly perfection upon our death. Perhaps You are calling us, rather, to an earthly perfection. How proud this sounds! But I feel the pull.

Your calling suggests a different form of perfection—one that accepts and transcends our flaws and failings. It's not an edict to achieve the impossible but an invitation to live in persistent humility, similar to how St. Paul directs us to pray without ceasing.[40] The "strangest commandment" invites us to a life of perfect imperfection. And when I understand You correctly, Lord, there is no longer any room for my pride—for all I am and have, every perfection which I enjoy, is Your doing, carving Your life into mine.

This is why perfection for these "humbled bones"[41] is the humble acceptance of our imperfection before Your perfection. It is here that perfect devotion is found, the perfect obedience to the first commandment etched in stone on Mt. Sinai by Your divine finger.[42] It is here that I can live a life without an iota of idolatry, for I shall have no false gods besides Thee. It's not a demand to change my nature, to have perfect knowledge or power, or even to be without fault.

---

39 See Matt. 7:7–8.

40 1 Thess. 5:16–18.

41 See Psalm 50:10.

42 See Exodus 20:1–3.

Rather, it is a call to forever live with a contrite heart before Thee, to recognize without ceasing that You are God and I am not. In this way, we can be perfectly imperfect. And it is upon this foundation of rock[43] that Your grace can elevate me, Your unworthy servant, to a mystical union with You, a *theosis* within You, surpassing all the abilities and powers of my will.

43 See Matt. 7:24–27.

XVII
Your Mystical Body Bleeds Still
or
The Bread of Life Discourse

(John 6)

O Lord, I seek insight that transcends the obvious. I seek to know You more intimately. Yet a question stirs in my heart: How much of my motive is pure? How much springs from the well of pride, seeking to drink in some unique insight to refresh my self-righteous heart? Can it be both?

I do not know the answer. And yet You grace me still—despite my pride, my sinfulness—with something I had not seen before; an insight revealing itself like the delicate petals of the morning glories in my wife's garden, how they unfold to greet the dawn.

As Your devoted followers know, You take on the form of lowly bread. What a sublime paradox! The Infinite contained within the finite, the Almighty cradled in mortal hands. The Fathers and Doctors of the Church have marveled at this supreme act of humility. They rightly marvel, as I do, that You became a speck of food, manhandled, gnawed, and consumed, yet every mortal falls short of capturing the full measure of Your humility. A lifetime of meditation could not comprehend, nor an eternity of poets crafting verse could articulate the meekness and humility of transubstantiation.

But my restless mind sought something other than I had considered before. I turned to the Gospel of John, Chapter 6, where the drama of Your revelation unfolds. The tension grows and grows as the multitude, having tasted Your miraculous power over the loaves and fishes, hungers for more.[44] An unimaginable power: that of multiplying food! They would surely crown You king by force, for they knew not the kingdom of which You spoke. I cannot blame them. What worldly kingdom can wield this power? To fill the bellies of one's subjects without time and toil, without seasons and sufferings? It is mightier than all the armies of every empire.

You flee to the solitude of the mountains and later tread upon the waters as if they were firm ground. The crowd, insatiable, pursues You still. Whether it be their doubt or grumbling bellies after a single day's passing, they demanded even more signs like the manna given by Moses.[45]

44 See John 6:1–15.

45 See John 6:30–31.

The perfect opportunity presents itself. They asked about bread of heaven. It is time for you to explain the toughest of Your teachings, knowing full well it would drive many away. But it's as if You orchestrated each of the notes in this symphony of revelation.

Trogo—Greek, meaning to chew, to gnaw upon Your very flesh.[46] How grotesque this seemed to some, how confounding it seemed to all. Yet You lead them gently toward understanding like a mother guiding her child's first steps. You eased the vulgarity by saying Your very same body would ascend to heaven and that the flesh profits nothing and that the words You spoke were spirit and life.[47] At least now they knew You didn't mean that you would sever flesh into tiny pieces and force them to eat it. Something else was at play, though they knew not what. How can one blame them? You asked for faith, but this, my Lord, was a tall ask. There is a meekness in allowing Your followers to remain in confusion, for pride (like mine) often requires being perfectly understood correctly at every moment.

Although the path to transubstantiation has not been fully revealed, we can see the groundwork being laid: the "supersubstantial bread" in the Lord's Prayer[48] to this bread of life discourse, culminating in the holy mystery of the Last Supper.

---

46 See John 6:24.

47 See John 6:63–64.

48 Matt. 6:11.

Yet for many of Your followers, it proves too much to bear. They turn away, their departure marked by that ominous verse—John 6:66.

Finally, O Lord, we arrive at the heart of Your meekness and humility: this scene, a foreshadowing of countless souls, millions upon millions, who would sever their ties with the twelve—the remnant, the true apostolic succession. How gentle Your spirit, how humble Your heart, to allow so many to turn from the precious Sacrament.

What divine patience! You watched Your greatest gift of self slowly and deliberately fade from the hearts of so many who claim Your name. Like petals falling from a flower, each denial a silent mourning.

Humbly, You witnessed Martin Luther's subtle assault on the great mystery of transubstantiation, his "consubstantiation" a whisper of doubt in the ears of the faithful. This marked the first tremor, echoing the footsteps of those who shook their heads and walked away from Your Bread of Life discourse so long before.

Then came Ulrich Zwingli reducing Your presence to mere symbol, and John Calvin seeking some middle ground by claiming Your true spiritual presence but no substance of flesh and blood. How many more slipped away, choosing an easier path? The damage is done. The demons rejoice.

Through the ages, the belief in the Sacrament drifted down like leaves carried away by autumn winds.

Truly, Your Church has been cut into pieces. The Body of Your Church, Your Mystical Body, lies severed from itself while Lucifer and his legion circle like vultures.

O, the bitter irony, Lord! The Body of Your Church torn asunder over the very question of whether Your flesh is torn asunder. In my pride, I rush to correct the slightest misunderstanding of my own words; yet You, in Your infinite meekness and humility allow even villains to rip your teachings apart.

Your Church, Lord God, in these countless divisions, has become another lamb led to slaughter. Your mystical body bleeds over the very issue of Your body and blood.

Lord, in Your boundless mercy, forgive them, for they know not what they do.

XVIII
Touching the Untouchable *or* Cleansing of the Leper

(Matthew 8:1–4)

Lord, I spent my life looking at the moments of Your life as if through a straw. Yet now, in my search of Your lessons in meekness and humility, I marvel at the seamless context of Your words and works. Everything is connected, a pattern of divine beauty, a technicolor coat woven for me, Your unworthy servant, to don with the pride of a prince. Nothing You said or did stands alone. You never sang a single note, but rather a celestial chorus, angels dancing on every verse. It is only through prayer that Your masterpiece is seen and heard and felt. These humble words are as dry bones. I cannot express the place You have taken my heart.

In the wake of Your great Sermon on the Mount, a sea of followers, with minds in wonder and hearts ablaze, desire all the more of you. They understand mere fragments of

Your words but are certain they come from a place of authority. While the blustering of Pharisees and Scribes[49] trap the common man in a labyrinth of 613 rules and rituals, You teach not as one who ensnares, but as one who liberates, "having power."[50]

It is now time for them to see this power.

What better way, I now see O Lord, than to show them a living, breathing example of how the poor in spirit, those who mourn, and the meek, will be blessed beyond compare. You orchestrated this miracle with more precision than Mozart crafted a crescendo.

As You descend the mount, I now see the suspense rising, the air thick with anticipation. Your sermon is not over. The climax is just in reach. And then, cries of delight turn to screeches of horror. The crowd parts like the Red Sea.

A leper emerges from the crowd.

A man humbled by weakness, disease, from being an outcast, approaches You. He is poor in spirit, for he has no pride left, no self-reliance. He relies on You alone. He mourns, and You desire to comfort him. He is meek, and thus beckons the inheritance You offer.

He is not interested in attaining Your power; he needs Your power. What a difference, O Lord.

In reading, I am among this crowd. In my own pride, I often stand with them looking for miracles, an outstretched hand for daily bread, yearning to be part of a movement

---

49 See Matt. 7:28.

50 Matt. 7:29.

toward victory. Yet in truth, I am as desperate as a leper, my soul corroded by sin rather than my flesh by disease. Though I walk freely among my family and friends, I risk becoming an eternal outcast, exiled from Your kingdom.

Here, amid the departing crowd, this humble man "adores" you. With the simplest, most profound expression—a hymn of doubtless faith and angelic certitude—this broken man gives life to the prayer you just taught Your disciples to pray. He adores You first and then says, "Lord, if thou wilt, thou canst make me clean."[51]

And You will it.

Moved by his unwavering truth, You reach out Your immaculate hand—the hand once held by the Virgin as You learned to walk, that would later multiply loaves and fishes, that would confer the Great Sacrament at the Last Supper, and would be pierced by a nail.

You touch the untouchable.[52]

Here, merciful Lord, the incarnation comes to mind as a touching of the untouchable. You left the throne of heaven to take on flesh, truly considered untouchable by Lucifer and his legions. If You were willing to bridge the chasm of the sacred and profane, why should I marvel at Your spotless hand touching a leper?

Yet the narrative unfolds further! How, O Master Weaver, have I not seen the leper as interwoven with the very next verse? Take away this straw through which I see Your

51 Matt. 8:2.

52 See Matthew 8:3.

life. Brighten the stories with Your light that I may see more clearly.

Foolishly, Lord Jesus, I had never noticed that after You cleanse the leper, You are confronted by another untouchable, a Roman centurion.[53] Again, You are confronted with a complete faith, one that makes You "marvel"—a notion worthy of its own reflection. He knew he was unworthy to have You even under his roof.

In both cases, humility of the untouchables moves Your humility from lesson into action.

Give me the grace, Lord, to see myself as an untouchable, for I know with complete certitude that if I attained this humility, then Your immaculate hand would reach out and touch my unclean soul.

---

53 See Matthew 8:5.

XIX
Jesus Marveled
or
The Centurion's Faith

(Matthew 8:5–13; Luke 7:1–10)

The more of Your humanity I behold, the more my affection grows, O Lord. Is this wrong? Are these emotions of mine an omen of faltering faith, seeking solace in Your humanity? Should it not be Your divine essence that jolts my soul into conversion, that ignites the fervor within my chest, that captivates my imagination? Is it that I long to worship one who reflects my own nature? Is Your humanity merely a smaller leap for my faith? Is Your divinity too daunting, too radiant for my eyes to gaze upon?

O Lord, Incarnate Word, it feels as if Your humanity glides past Your divinity—the finite eclipsing the infinite, leaving but a halo around the edge of my understanding.

I pen these thoughts on April 8, 2024, a day marked by a solar eclipse. We will use glasses to shield our sight, for even an eclipse star is too overwhelming for our mortal eyes. In similar manner, I feel Your eclipsed divinity—the Son cloaked with humanity—is too magnificent for my gaze. Yet Your humanity renders it bearable. We can look upon You in wonder and awe. We echo the words of the centurion: "Lord, I am not worthy that You should enter under my roof."[54]

I wander down this path, O Lord, because there are moments when You humbly reveal Your humanity to me with profound clarity. When You weep at Lazarus's tomb, Your humanity cries out to my soul. When Your righteous anger defends the sanctity of Your Father's house, I feel my heart beat quicken, ready to defend His honor. And when You cried out on the cross in the agony of isolation "Eli, Eli, lama sabachthani?": in the groans of Your humanity, I hear my own voice. And hope arises within my heart.

Here, in Matthew 8 and Luke 7, You grant me another peak into Your glorious humanity: "And Jesus hearing this, marveled." You marveled, O Lord? In these sacred moments, Your humanity must have eclipsed Your divinity. The All-Knowing was surprised? The All-Powerful was astounded? You, the Unmoved Mover, were moved? How can a sinful man—a mere creature molded from the dust of the Earth—cause the infinite person of Jesus Christ to marvel?

---

54 Matt. 8:8.

A man of earthly command, accustomed to instant obedience, recognizing a power greater than Caesar's. He understood power.

Luke's Gospel further illuminates his humility as he sent Jewish leaders to catch Your attention, believing that You would overlook a Roman soldier. Then he sent friends to prevent You from entering his house; he felt unworthy.[55] These mediators were not sent out of laziness but from a profound recognition of his unworthiness to approach You and certainly to have You under his roof.

He sought no grandeur or spectacle. His request was void of self-interest. He simply loved his servant and sought healing for him. "Amen I say to you," You said to Your followers, those who had lived under the blade of Roman persecution every day of their lives. "I have not found so great faith, not even in Israel."[56]

You marveled.

How, O Lord, can I bring forth wonder in You? How might I move You, astonish You, catch Your immaculate heart off guard? Can I cause it to skip a beat?

If I lived as long as the Old Testament patriarchs, even 930 years as Adam, 912 years as Seth, 905 as Enos, or even 950 as Noah himself, with the sole purpose of marveling You, I would not do so by conquering the world, converting millions, erecting mighty cathedrals or gathering throngs of people to worship You therein. Not even if I

---

55 See Luke 7:1–7.

56 Luke 7:9.

filled the belly of every starving child, visited every captive in prison, clothed the masses shivering in the shadows of destitution. None of these triumphs would cause You to marvel without a humble and contrite heart beating within my breast—a heart that knows with the centurion's certitude that I remain unworthy to have You under my roof.

XX

Writing on the Ground *or* The Woman Caught in Adultery

(John 8:1–11)

Lord, what were Your teachings in the temple when the Scribes and Pharisees barged in with their trial and trickery? Were You speaking of the beatitudes, the hypocrisy of legalism, or at the climax of a parable, thus preventing it from being etched in Scripture?

Forgive me if my imagination runs too wild. Perhaps You were depicting the story of a young girl, a mere teenager, cruelly given in marriage to an old man, wicked in his carnal passions and domestic demands. And some years later, the girl became a woman and captured the attention of a man her own age. He was kind to her, gentle, and a genuine romance blossomed just as the cruelty of her spouse climaxed.

In her longing for affection amidst the suffering of abuse, she sought sinful solace in the embrace of this young man instead of divine providence. It was then that they were discovered, her husband leading the charge to stone her.

Lord, my imagination could never guess Your exact words before she was dragged before You. And yet, I can easily believe they were a perfect foreshadowing of what was to come. Your timing is too perfect to be otherwise. And so, I imagine Your audience was hearing something akin to this sad story of a young woman when that brood of vipers presented the adulteress before You.

These devious men, seeking to entrap You, invoked the law of Moses, conspicuously omitting the adulterating partner required by law to be brought forth. If she were caught in adultery, surely there was another. Who was he? Was he the young lover from the story I imagined, cowering behind a pillar, witnessing in terror as his beloved was condemned, his heart erupting with regret and shame? Or was he an older, influential man who could bribe his accusers? Or was he among the accusers, a privileged legalist protecting his own reputation—his gold coins spilling from the woman's scrip as she was cast to the ground, rolling to where You would write in the dust.

My thoughts, O Lord, are haunted by these possibilities.

I confess, Lord, if this woman were a veteran of the night, was she less deserving of mercy? But if she was a young victim, beautiful in youth, burdened with abuse, in love with he who could liberate her from a terrorizing spouse, a child of God ensnared in the sins of man, my sympathy spills over the damn of judgment.

My imagination paints these two extremes of the moral spectrum. Yet Your grace slices through such dichotomies, revealing the truth. In the stillness of my heart I hear You say, "These women are one and the same, divided only by time." To my pharisaical soul, I see a hardened harlot of the night, but You, Lord, see a frightened young girl crying for help.

How often we judge a criminal, wicked in every way, forgetting he was once an innocent child, seeking love and affection, only to be met with hatred and indifference. It is humility that opens our eyes to see how we and others are shaped by our environment. How, O Lord, can I boast of my achievements when they stem from countless blessings? If I had been born in a squalid alleyway in Calcutta to a mother in prostitution, never experiencing familial warmth, never crossing the threshold of a church, fighting daily to survive—what would my accomplishments be? How fervent would my prayers be? How often would I contemplate Your life? How much moral merit could I possibly have, given the undeserved life of abundant love and grace?

The woman thrown down before You is deserving of compassion, irrespective of her past. This much I am certain of. Remove the stone from my heart; let me cast it not on any other.

As the Scribes and Pharisees commenced their deceit, what did You stoop down to write? I've heard theories of

Your writing out their sins, making them slink away in shame. Yet my studies suggest it might relate more closely to Jeremiah 17:13: "O Lord, the hope of Israel, all that forsake thee shall be confounded, they that depart from thee, shall be written in the earth, because they have forsaken the Lord, the vein of living water." Was it prophetic, Lord? The tradition they knew well was to present both adulterers before the priest. Then he would stoop down and with his finger in the dust of the temple floor, write the law that had been broken alongside the names of the accused. Were You, Lord, inscribing their names as lawbreakers for failing to bring both adulterers, a creative indictment of their hypocrisy? Thus, they were unwilling to cast the first stone.

O, how we long to point fingers and accuse others and yet expect mercy for ourselves. But in Your meekness, You refrained from broadcasting their sins aloud, which You could have done to expose their hypocrisy. Instead, just writing in the dust sufficed. They left in shame, as Jeremiah had prophesied—not out of remorse but out of frustration, a strategic withdrawal to muster strength for future confrontations.

You approached the woman. I envision her gazing into Your merciful eyes—eyes of humility that also look upon me daily, Lord. And I hear Your voice echoing, "Go, and sin no more."

"Learn from me, for I am meek and humble of heart." If I can regard others with such compassion, will You not behold me with the same mercy on my judgment day?

XXI
The Rising of Matthew
or
The Calling of Matthew

(Matthew 9:9–13; Mark 2:14–17)

Who is my Matthew, O Lord? You chose him for reasons as numerous as the stars. Your choices are simple, for they are unencumbered with the duplicity that complicates my own decisions. And yet, Your choices seemingly have infinite rationales and consequences, for You see the causes of earthly actions stretching back to the beginning of time and the eternal consequences of our every move. You calculate the myriad outcomes rolling through the ages of every word You utter and step You take. And so, did You choose him, the tax collector, the sinner, the traitor, the collaborator, the embezzler, for one simple reason or for one reason for each soul touched by Your Gospel?

Your humility arises off the pages of Scripture as Matthew arose from his table to follow You. Yet again, I now see the beautiful context in which You work. Nothing with You is in a vacuum. You orchestrate all things perfectly. I now see, Lord Jesus, Matthew arising from his coin-laden table in light of the paralytic You lifted from his mat just two verses ago. How did I never see the connection before?

The limbs of the paralytic were twisted, contorted, and he was stuck on his mat. Upon Your word "Arise," the palsy's joints and muscles and tendons loosened, straightened out, and he arose. A rising for the ages. A healing of rare spectacle for all to see for the sake of giving glory to God. He arose, took up his bed, and went away.[57] It seems, Lord, the last thing he would want to do was take his nasty mat with him, for he could now leave his crippled past behind. Yet it was precisely this mat that informs the Jews that this was the cripple.[58] Do You, Lord, allow us to carry our "past" to enable us to evangelize and profess Your mercy and providence?

Yes, the paralytic went along his way, and You went along Your way. And there You were, simply passing by Matthew's table, while the impact of Your miracles rippled through the crowds. You had just scandalized the Scribes by declaring the paralytic's sins forgiven and commanding his healing—a spectacle of divine authority that now set the stage for Matthew's calling.

---

57 See Matt. 9:7.

58 See John 5:10.

"And when Jesus passed from thence, he saw a man named Matthew sitting at the custom house."[59] Here, O Lord, I see a man whose soul is as twisted and contorted with greed, far more grotesque than the body of the cripple. A Jew, haunted by the faith of his childhood, now aligned with the occupying Romans, enriching himself by betrayal, skimming off the top, squeezing the downtrodden of their scarcity to pad his abundance. He was a daily Judas to Your chosen people.

Perhaps as a child, You witnessed such men while standing in line with Joseph to pay taxes. I imagine Joseph teaching You about forgiveness and patience in the face of extortion by tax collectors. As a young man, knowledgeable in worldly affairs, You surely did Your own calculations of the modest profits needed to sustain Yourself and Your mother; Your almsgiving, all while observing a greedy man manipulating scales with a look that said, "We all know the truth, and there's nothing you can do about it." Perhaps these memories flooded Your mind as Your eyes connected with Levi, son of Alpheus, sitting in the custom house.

But You, in Your infinite wisdom and humility, saw in Matthew a man much like the paralytic who garnered compassion from all who saw his affliction. You saw Matthew's twisted soul and Your compassion overflowed, just as it did upon healing the paralytic. With that same compassion, You saw his constant sorrow, his alienation from his people, his buried guilt and shame.

---

[59] Matt. 9:9.

Your eyes fixed on him. How long did You look? Did You smile? Was it a look of authority, something this man would know? Was it a look of mercy, something this man would not know? Did You point as Caravaggio depicts, or did You simply say, "Follow me"?

As "arise" breathed life into the withered limbs of the palsy, so too does "follow me" breathe life into Matthew's heart. His grip on greed loosened, his soul straightened out, and he arose and followed. There was no spectacle as with the palsy, no cheering crowds, at least on earth. Yet the angels sang glorious hymns of celebration for the healing of this crooked soul. It may not have garnered the attention of the crowds, but it was a profundity worthy of the greatest painters, poets and preachers.

Your closest followers must have been dismayed, scandalized, perhaps enraged. To walk with a tax collector, to talk with him, to befriend him! You ask, O Lord, so little and so much of us at the same time. Your yoke is easy, but how heavy we make it with our own prejudices and preconceptions.

To make Your motives unmistakably clear, You accepted Matthew's invitation to dine at his house, a move You likely orchestrated. The discomfort of Your followers, crammed into the tax collector's home beside more sinners, makes me chuckle. But it was no laughing matter to them, nor to the watching Pharisees who questioned them. I imagine Your intervention was swift because Your little ones had no idea how to explain this utter disregard for societal norms. It would take them time.

As You often did with the rigid Pharisees, Your simple yet profound response transcended conventional wisdom: "They that are in health need not a physician, but they that are ill."[60] With the gentleness of a doctor stooping down to clean the wounds of a man riddled with infection, You ministered not only to the publicans and sinners but also to Your disciples and the guardians of the law, stiff in their spiritual limbs as the paralytic had been in his physical ones.

You offered one final instruction, quoting Hosea: "For I desired mercy, and not sacrifice."[61] You taught mercy by being merciful, showing that God no longer desires blood sacrifice, but humble and merciful hearts.

Who then, Lord Jesus, is my Matthew? How has my own heart stiffened like the paralytic's limbs? Whom have You placed in my path that needs my mercy, or more so, whom must I show mercy to? Who are the tax collectors and sinners with whom I refuse to dine due to self-righteousness?

Who is my Matthew?

60 Matt. 9:12.

61 Osee 6:6.

XXII
The One Thing Martha Lacked
or
Mary and Martha

(Luke 10:38–42)

Martha, Martha, Martha. Peace. Be still. In the quiet of my prayer, I see the turbulent waters of chores and tasks thrashing Martha, tossing her relentlessly, her spirit on the brink of capsizing into the depths of anxiety. All of us have been there. Some of us live there.

Lord Jesus, sovereign of tranquility, I am bewildered at people's effort to vindicate Martha, to rationalize away Your tender admonition. With humility, Lord, I ask: Why have even some of Your saints portrayed her as representing one of the two paths—the active alongside the contemplative? Though interpretations abound, one truth emerges: Martha was wrong. Mary was right. There is an arrogance entangling the active soul, the hard worker man, the duty-bound woman, the industrious spirit so prized by our hyperactive world. "I'm a Martha," they proudly say, unconscious of the unsightly comparison.

Here is the point of the Mary and Martha story: there is a season for action and a season for prayer, yet never a season for anxiety.

This was Your gentle rebuke. You did not denounce work. You denounce worry, anxiety, tension, antagonism, judgment, self-righteousness, all of which are seen in Martha's words and actions. And yet we proudly proclaim, "I'm a Martha"? Indeed, I am at times a Martha, for we all are. Yet this should be a title of shame, not honor.

It is as if You instructed Martha: *Learn from Mary, for she is meek and humble of heart*. Her humility was not merely in her physical posture before You, but in her tranquil spirit during daily chores. Mary found her solace in You, whether seated at Your feet or amidst kitchen labors. Mary's devotion did not preclude work, but Martha's work precluded devotion. There was too much to do. Just too much to do.

Then You say, "Martha, Martha, thou art careful and art troubled about many things: but one thing is necessary."[62] So, what was this one thing Martha lacked, O Lord?

Your teachings cascade from the scriptures like water meandering down a gentle stream. Your words seamlessly flowing into one another, carrying the vital current of revelation.

Only a few lines before in Luke 10, we find the ebbing waters of the Good Samaritan, the principal model of the

---

62 Luke 10:41–42.

active life, diligently serving the lonely man beaten by robbers. Indeed, Lord, You cherish Your laborers. You did not rebuke the Samaritan's choice to act rather than to merely pray for the injured man. In stark contrast, the priest and the Levite, epitomes of the contemplative life, are portrayed as embodiments of pride and hypocrisy. It is the outcast, he who was unafraid to soil his hands, whom You commend.

But what was the deeper intent behind this parable? We must delve further upstream, sensing the currents of truth that swirl about us. You told this parable in response to the scholar who tested You with the question, "What must I do to possess eternal life?"[63] In a divine reversal, You asked him to reflect on his own understanding. Regardless of whether he was consumed by pride, he recited the perfect answer: "Thou shalt love the Lord thy God with thy whole heart, and with thy whole soul, and with all thy strength, and with all thy mind; and thy neighbor as thyself."[64] His follow-up question, "Who is my neighbor?"[65] led You to tell of the man beaten and abandoned—this is his neighbor.

The currents of this story seamlessly flow into the story of Mary and Martha. I can visualize the scene: "Martha was busy about much serving."[66] Perhaps it involved food; other translations suggest "busy with preparations." The Greek term *diakonia* typically refers to the administration

63 Luke 10:25.
64 Luke 10:27.
65 Luke 10:29.
66 Luke 10:40.

of duties. Conceivably, Martha was orchestrating logistics for Your upcoming engagements or preparing provisions for Your disciples. In any event, she was bustling about, her footsteps growing louder with frustration, throwing impatient glares at Mary which said, "There is too much to do for you to sit there. Just too much to do!"

Martha's frustration reached a peak, causing a scene. She "stood" Scripture says, which seems to mean stood amidst those who were gathered around You, directing all attention from You to herself. In other words, she barged in. I envision her fists clenched at her hips, the disciples awkwardly diverting their gaze. Not only did she voice her displeasure, but she aired her complaint about Mary in front of everyone! Imagine, a room filled with men witnessing her outburst. Was her indignation so profound that it screamed, "Look at me! And look at her!"?

Yet, in Your response, You teach us much, notably how to respond to one making a fuss, how respond to pride with humility.

"Martha, Martha." You gently calmed her down. You reminded her, and all of us, that only one thing is essential. I trust, Lord, that this "one thing" is akin to what is required to inherit eternal life: to love God wholly and completely, taking us back up stream to the scholar's question, "What must I do to inherit eternal life." And if we truly embrace the first commandment, then the second naturally flows. The sisters' tale reflects the essence of Your greatest commandment, showing how devotion to God naturally leads to compassion for others. And the current continues to flow.

Right after we behold the young Mary, the mother of the contemplative life, You give us the perfect prayer, the *Pater Noster*. You emphasize trustful surrender in this prayer, reassuring us that God will meet our needs. "Ask, and it shall be given you: seek, and you shall find: knock, and it shall be opened to you . . . And which of you, if he ask his father bread, will he give him a stone?"[67] It is as if You are still speaking to Martha in each of us.

The Father will provide all we need for eternal life. But we must continually seek, persistently ask. You are showing us that our hearts must rest at Your feet, Lord Jesus, even if our feet must move, our hands labor, and our minds solve problems. Our hearts must be silent, even if our minds race and our mouths run. Our hearts must stay calm, even as we toil amid the demands of service.

No, Lord, we cannot justify Martha's approach. She erred, overtaken by pride that led to her public display.

If we embody meekness and humility like You, we will perform our duties while our hearts remain with Mary at Your feet, loving You with all our heart, soul, strength, and mind. We will readily aid the downtrodden and abandoned.

You are the one thing necessary. If we focus on You, surely all that we need to do Your will shall be laid before us.

There is a time for work. There is a time for prayer. There is never time for anxiety.

---

67 Luke 11:9–11.

XXIII
Sitting at Abba's Feet
or
The Lord's Prayer

(Luke 10:42–11:4; Matthew 6:9–13)

O Lord, my God, how blind I have been to the divine fabric of Your Word. It weaves through the text, forming a beautiful pattern, one that can only be seen by stepping back and seeing the greater image. Never again shall I presume to grasp a verse in isolation. Truly, the sequence of Your life's story in the words of the evangelists is not merely brilliant, but divinely orchestrated.

How beautiful, O Lord, when I realized that Your immaculate words to Martha about Mary are one verse before Your lesson in how to pray. The chapter break has blocked my understanding for decades. It cannot be coincidence that You say about Mary who sits at Your feet in tranquility, "One thing is necessary. Mary has chosen the better part, which shall not be taken away from her."[68] And the very next verse Your disciples ask, "Lord, teach us to pray."[69] I think if that chapter break had not been there, we would have seen Mary's serenity as an introit of sorts, an overture to the greatest prayer ever taught.

Before us are two sisters: Martha, consumed by anxious toil and anger and self-righteousness, and Mary, calm and single-minded and humble, a picture of tranquil devotion. In her silence and stillness, we behold the essence of mental prayer—the mother of all contemplatives. She at Your feet, her soul soaking in Your presence, foreshadowing the moment she will soak Your feet with precious ointment and tears.

It is in this spirit of meekness and humility that we must approach You, O Lord. Only then can the words You gave us truly spring from our lips and leap from our heart to the ears of Your Father.

"Lord, teach us to pray," a verse so well loved, echoing through the ages. Yet how often we forget its completion: "as John also taught his disciples." O, that I might know the prayer of John, greatest of prophets, of whom You said, "Among those born of women, there has not risen anyone greater than John the Baptist."[70]

What might John's prayers have been like? Can we see glimmers of them in the ecstasy of saints? Can we hear

---

68 Luke 10:42.

69 Luke 11:1.

70 Luke 7:28.

whispers of them in the moans of desert fathers, battling the legions of hell? What precious words flowed from the lips of Your great herald? Were they striking in their eloquence or poetic in their simplicity?

Though the precise words escape our grasp, we can be certain that John's prayers were ignited by the fire of humility.

Perhaps it began with a solemn invocation like one of David's psalms: "To Thee have I lifted up my eyes, who dwellest in heaven."[71] But it would have lacked the tenderness that You, O Lord, gave us with the words "Our Father," or more tenderly still, "Abba." You, who alone can claim sonship and proclaim "My Father" draws us into Your sacred relationship, bridging the infinite chasm between mortal and divine. Even for the Baptist, this chasm may have appeared too vast to cross. Would he have dared call Your Father "Abba"? Perhaps You taught him, or better yet, gave Him permission to do so as young men, or even boys.

John knew the Old Testament well. He knew the concept of God as Father was present, though it was a distant, nebulous notion. Israel was proclaimed God's firstborn,[72] and God said to Solomon, "I will be a father to him, and he shall be a son to me."[73] Isaiah, too, occasionally alluded to God as Father, though more in the sense of Creator and Maker.[74]

---

71 Ps. 122:1.

72 Ex. 4:22–23.

73 2 Sm 7:14 (NRSVCE).

74 Is. 63:16; 64:8.

Even David hinted at God's paternal nature as the "father of orphans."[75]

But "Abba"?

Your persistent, seemingly impertinent reference to "My Father in heaven" must have rubbed Your sceptics wrong, and perhaps Your friends as well. To feel the great divide between man and God was bred into their very emotions.

Yet, in Your divine humility, You draw heaven toward earth. Through Your grace, You lift us heavenward. It is through You that *Your* Abba became *our* Abba.

Our *Abba, Abba*. What a childlike word. Who among us is man enough to call Him *Daddy*?[76] *Daddy*. A word I hear so often. A word I so often ignore amidst the chaos of family life. Yet my heart knows I will miss it soon enough. The *Daddy* slowly becomes *Dad*, but that one little syllable missing is a small death. But through You, O Lord, we are elevated through Your grace; no longer do we each think of "my father," for God becomes "Our Father." We join in Your familial union.

Now we, His children, may sit at His feet, soaking in His fatherhood, just as Mary sat at Your feet, soaking in Your presence. In this sacred intimacy, we find the essence of prayer, the heart of our relationship with our Father, who art in heaven.

---

75 Ps. 67:5.

76 Matt. 18:3.

XXIV

Passing to the Other Side *or* The Calming of the Storm

(Mark 4:35–40)

Let us pass over to the other side.[77] Yes, indeed, Lord. It is long past time for me to pass to the other side. With my feet sinking in the sands of the shore, I look across the sea of divine providence, ebbing, thrashing, crashing. I step slowly toward Your boat, like a child on the edge of a pool, fearful to leave safety's edge.

Will You care if I perish? Do You call me to perish?

As I prayed this passage, wrote about this passage, spoke of this passage, more times than I can recall, I see it has less to do with You calming the storm and more to do with You calming my heart.

77 Mark 4:35.

So meekly You laid in the boat's stern. And I see music. The beating winds and violent waves lulled You to sleep, like a baby listening to a lullaby in Mary's arms. Whereas the apostles felt anxiety and stress, burdens and threats, You see the Divine Conductor leading all instruments to sing out their own notes in perfect harmony. Like the apostles, I feel the chaos of swirling waves and cry out, "Do you not care if we perish?"[78]; yet You see harmony of purpose and circumstance. When I feel the dread of drowning and the cacophony of confusion, You hear the melody of the Divine Symphony.

Truly, O Lord, it is time for me to pass over to the other side.

It is my pride that yells out my impending doom. "Do You not care if I perish? Do You not care? Am I not more valuable than this? Do I not deserve better than to suffer these trials? Are not I with You so that You can save me?"

Ah! And there we have it. I want Your wonders more than You. Would I rather a calm sea with You on the shore, or thunderous skies, tumultuous waves, ever expecting the dark waters to swallow me whole, but with You asleep in my boat? Do I possess the humility to be at peace, to be still amidst the storm? Can I keep my little ones calm? My bride calm? My friends? Or will my frenetic pride rile my passengers to their own despair?

Humility brings calm while pride leads to frenzy; meekness fosters peace, but aggression incites anger.

---

78 Mark 4:38 (RSV).

It is time to pass over to the other side.

The waters have only the power over me that You give them. If my lungs are filled with them, it is because You make it so. If I sink into their abyss, slowly watching the light above fade to black, it is You who pull me down. Can I rest as the light slips away? Can I be at peace as You were in the boat?

Slowly sinking, ever deeper, ever darker, might be my passing to the other side.

Am I ready?

Is it on my terms, O Lord, or Yours? Is my discipleship conditional? Will I yell at You to awake, to bail water, to hold the mast, to do Your fair share? Will I demand a miracle in exchange for my fidelity?

O Jesus Christ, Son of the living God, let the storm pass from me. But not my will, but thine be done. I hear you call, "Peace, be still."

It is time to pass over to the other side.

XXV
Into the Hills
or
The Multiplication of Loaves and Fishes

(John 6:1–15)

My Lord and my God, I am no different from those wayward souls You came to redeem two millennia past. Even after the flourishing tree has branched forth, the fruit of Your Church has ripened, the flowers of Your grace have blossomed, I, weak in faith, still seek Your miracles to satiate my hunger.

O, truly my belly overflows. Yet still I clamor to swell my coffers, alleviate my suffering, enhance my ease, and expand my dominion. Yes, indeed, Lord, You reign as my King—as long as my belly remains full.

As I delve into Your sacred text, I witness Your compassion for humanity. I see You lift Your eyes to heaven, giving thanks to Your Father. I see the miracle. I see how You can multiply talents in myriad ways. And I realize that I am but a fragment, gathered up among the twelve baskets, representing the twelve tribes of Israel, the twelve apostles, and Your holy Catholic and Apostolic Church. Here lies the vastness of Your plan, nestled deep within Your sacred Church.

These beautiful symbolisms mark a pivotal event in Your life, but it is the following passage, O Lord, that truly proclaims Your humility and meekness.

John 6:14–15 speaks directly to me, I confess. Like those misguided men, I desire a king of this world—a new David, a Messiah who will satiate every hunger on earth, wielding miraculous power to vanquish the foes of God. At times, my heart burns with zeal. And You feared that we might seize You by force, thrusting You onto a throne, crowning You with gold. Jesus Christ, the Lamb led to slaughter, I now understand that a crown of jewels would inflict greater torment on You than a crown of thorns. Your kingdom is not of this world.

You see me approaching, zeal blazing in my eyes, reprisal on my mind, and You retreat into the hills. You evade me, Lord. My presence drives You away. You flee to the solitude of the mountains, seeking the company of Your Father.

You run because I pursue not who You truly are, but who I desire You to be.

Stay, Lord. I no longer pursue. My belly is empty, and I seek nothing to fill it. My pain is intense, yet I accept it. I ask for no miracles, no loaves nor fishes. I desire nothing of this world. I ask only for You, that You might lead me into the hills to be with Your Father.

XXVI
Leisure at Sea
or
The Walking on Water

(Matthew 14:20–33)

The twelve baskets of fragments remain as a symbol of this astounding, mesmerizing miracle. As You fed thousands with five loaves and two fish, so also did You gather the twelve tribes of Israel and establish Your Church with twelve apostles. I, Your unworthy servant, pray that I too be gathered up as a fragment into the basket of Your apostolic Church.

Yet, another lesson of Your meekness and humility gently unfolds before me. In the autumn of my years, with youth behind me, bearing the weight of countless missteps, embarrassments lodged in my memory, I understand the foolishness of Your apostles. I see myself in them and how they foolishly react to the spectacle of feeding thousands.

The feeding of the multitude stands as one of history's most extraordinary moments, rivaling the parting of the Red Sea and the fall of Jericho's walls. Food, glorious food, materialized from seemingly nothing. What power could rival this? No high priest could conjure up a tiny shrimp, no Caesar could make appear the smallest crumb. Yet You, with Your rabble of followers, fed the masses with a single prayer and gleaming eye toward Your Father in heaven.

The triumph of the moment was overwhelming. Your apostles', briming with adrenaline and wonder, must have overflowed with tears as the loaves weighed down their baskets, falling to their knees in awe.

You directed them to the boats and, curiously, remained with the multitude.[79] Upon dismissing the crowd, You retreated to the hills alone to pray.[80] I imagine Your apostles reclining in their boats, feasting on the fragments from the twelve baskets, indulging in wine, swapping stories of the day's marvels, belly laughter shaking the boat, echoed across the sea as they speculated on the worldly victories sure to follow such a display of mighty power.

Basking in the afterglow of Your glory, they were at leisure on the water.

Which man would sit on Your right and left? How many days remained for Roman occupation? What were the splendors to be of the Kingdom of God on Earth? Such

---

79 See Matt. 14:22.

80 See Matt. 14:23.

questions would be expected, particularly from the young and daring and zealous.

The young men celebrated with full bellies and grander dreams, hollering farewell to their enemies under the gleaming moonlight, the effects of wine in full swing, pushing each word and act a little further toward the absurd. All the while, You, my humble Lord, were alone in prayer, thanking Your Father and beseeching Him to enlighten the multitudes and Your apostles, to turn their focus inward and understand the true nature of the Messiah.

And so, You and Your Father decided to test the faith of these young men. A mighty wind jolted them from their revelry, tossing their boat with violent waves. After hours of useless struggle, in the fourth watch of the night, when celebration had given way to fear and exhaustion, they beheld You walking calmly, at leisure, across the raging waters.

The wind broke their faith within hours of it reaching a pitch. How flimsy was their resolve? How flimsy, O Lord, is mine?

And then, a moment of confusion breaks their fixation on disaster. I can hear them asking, "What is that? There! Right there!"

Out of the storm, the anxiety, the turmoil, You emerged, Master of the elements once again. You not only provide our daily bread but also pass through the tempests of our lives, bringing tranquility. The thrashing waters bite at Your heel as the serpent does at Your mother's, yet truly, O Lord, You crush the head of the storms in my life—the stressors, anxieties, uncertainties, and fears. You subdue these enemies of peace and invite me to step out of the boat, to walk upon these worldly trials, to place these earthly burdens beneath my feet. My feet? No Lord. My earthly burdens must be beneath Your feet. And Your grace can keep me afloat however long You wish.

With eyes upon You, my feet glide across this earthly life, but only to the extent that I become a member of Your Mystical Body. When I hear the raging winds, my faith falters. I forget Your countless demonstrations of divinity, becoming consumed by immediate concerns and fears, foolishly sinking into the belief that my efforts alone must keep me afloat.

There You stand, at leisure on the water amidst the storm, while I cling to my own strength, to my flimsy lifeboat. If only I too could be at leisure on the water, watching all the world frolic about with needless anxiety. But my boat is filled with worry. It is filled with doubt. Yet, O Lord, You call me to abandon the illusory security of my little boat and step into the storm. You bid me come and walk with You upon the water.

My pride must be left in the boat. I will let it tremble in fear as the coward that it is. With You, Lord, I will humbly walk amidst the storm, meekly across the waves, knowing that without meekness and humility, I will surely drown in the storms of life.

XXVII
Arise and Fear Not
or
The Transfiguration

(Matthew 17:1–9)

Thank you, Divine Master, for showing me something I had never seen before. Truly, communion with You in prayer transfigures all earthly wisdom, surpassing the loftiest thoughts, the most diligent studies. It is within the sacred realm of prayer that the veils of mystery are drawn back and insights are revealed to mortal eyes.

With a tinge of irony, this intimate communion with You reveals that Your transfiguration is about, of all things, communion with You. In my previous encounters with this luminous passage—Your face radiant as the noonday sun, Your garments white as snow—I was captivated merely by the spectacle of the miracle. But now, by Your grace, I perceive a deeper truth, namely, a sublime call to prayer. In response to, "Lord, teach us to pray," You bestowed on the world the perfect words, a divine love song to our heavenly Father. Yet here, upon this hallowed mountaintop, You impart not just words, but the very essence of how my spirit ought to move.

The journey of mental prayer begins with a withdrawal into solitude, with You, Lord, far from the cacophony of worldly concerns, rising above the tumult and clamor of our search for meaning on this mortal coil. I implore You, take my heart to the mountain top, to that sacred pinnacle, high above and far away.

After escaping the external noise of my life, grant me that interior silence necessary to behold You in Your glory. Until my heart is still in quiet, I will not rest in you, O Lord. Calm the storm of my passions, silence the winds of my memory, imagination, and speculation. Only then will I see the story of my salvation manifest before me as Your followers did on the mount: the prophets of old, one representing the eternal law of God etched in stone for weak-willed man, the other representing the timeless eternity awaiting me if I live by the covenant, both conversing with You forever; and You at the very center of it all. This is what they saw in Your transfiguration. This is what I am called to see in prayer.

In the midst of this wondrous exchange with You—my God, my Savior—Your form begins to fade. A luminous cloud overshadows me. I am bewildered. A deep and mighty voice resounds, mighty, menacing, ominous, "This is my beloved Son, in whom I am well pleased. Hear ye Him."[81] Truly, O Lord, meditation upon Your life inevitably leads to Your Father. Your Incarnation bridges the great gorge between divinity and humanity, a bridge that I tremble to cross, looking into the abyss between the boards that my feet traverse. But Your freely offered brotherhood renders You approachable. I more readily perceive Your voice, see Your face, and partake of Your flesh and blood beneath the humble guise of bread and wine—perhaps the only manifestation my frail nature can endure.

Yet You do not abandon me in this state for long. The Father makes His presence known, and all is transformed. I stand before the largeness of unmitigated divinity, graciously conformed to the smallness of humanity, and I am overwhelmed. Like Peter, James, and John before me, I prostrate myself, shielding my face, gripped by holy fear. Words fail me; thought itself flees.

Speech, sight, and strength desert me. All this, though I comprehend it not in the moment, forms a prayer of surpassing beauty.

Then, as I lie trembling, You reach down and touch me, and Your voice, gentle yet powerful, says, "Arise, and fear not."[82] I lift my gaze to find only You. The Father has withdrawn, having commanded me to listen to You. His words few yet profoundly giant. You raise me from the ground, granting me Your peace, and guide me down from the

---

81 Matt. 17:5.

82 Matt. 17:7.

mountain of prayer, back to the realm of mortality, enjoining me to keep this sacred encounter hidden for a time.

Your transfiguration, Lord Jesus, mirrors the story of my own transfiguration through prayer. In this contemplative state, if I am not moved by profound humility to cast myself down in reverent fear before the Lord God, Your Father, I deny both You and myself the blessed moment when You reach down to me, saying, "Arise, and fear not."

XXVIII
I Am Not Worthy
or
The Prodigal Son

(Luke 15:11–32)

A parable unparalleled in brilliance, O Lord. Its timeless truths echo through the ages, ringing as clear to us today as those of yesterday. Your wisdom weaves so much truth together, spreading open our imagination in myriad ways. We can cast ourselves as any character in this timeless tale.

As St. Ignatius taught us, we can, through the application of the senses, place ourselves in the story, Your story, our senses attuned to the divine message crafted just for us at this time.

I can easily cast myself as the prodigal son, with worldly desires, yearning for liberation from duty and constraint, craving the intoxicating allure of indulgence and ambition. Behold, the dusty road stretches before me, alive with bleating sheep and the alluring laughter from the city tavern.

With reckless abandon, I can easily throw myself into the muck and mire of uncontrolled passion, quickly exhausting the grace that has kept me safe all this time. In the mud with pigs, feeding from the trough is where I deserve to be, tasting the filth sliding down my throat.

Or I can be a new character in the story, a friend of the prodigal son, meeting him in the city, hearing the story of his wealth, but watching it slip through his fingers like sand, my words of caution falling on deaf ears. I watch him anxiously count his remaining coins, wondering where the rest have gone. I see his transformation from a vibrant youth into a mere shadow. Yet even in his darkest hour, I hope for his safe return home.

My Lord, I can easily play the role of the compassionate father, my heart rent by my son's request to take the money and run. Tears run down my face as he does toward his own destruction. My prayers ascend to heaven, for his safety, maturity, wisdom. The stars find me on the front porch every night, gazing down the lonely road, hoping for his return.

As a father, this is easy. How could I not suffer his departure? How could I not hope for and rejoice in his return? I fear meeting the father who does not.

But have I the humility to truly rejoice upon the return of a repentant sinner if he be not my own progeny? Or have I feasted, indulged, gorged on self-righteousness as the older son had? Do I compare the spiritual scorecard of others to my own? Am I ruthless in my judgment of others yet presumptuous of Your mercy for myself?

All of these angles of the story are well-known, are obvious at a cursory glance, O Lord. Yet, there is one passage that repeats itself that I have previously missed despite it being conspicuous to one who simply reads the words slowly and intentionally.

Merciful Jesus, I can easily relate to the prodigal son who throws himself to the winds of indulgence, who squanders his spiritual inheritance received in sacramental grace; yet I can also relate to his desire to seek forgiveness, to return home. But here is the looming question that haunts my soul: have I ever meant the words he uttered not once in this parable, but twice: "I am not worthy to be called your son."

How foolish my mind can be, reading this passage countless times, glossing over the lesson in humility. The prodigal son is so humbled by his failure that he truly feels unworthy to ever be considered his father's son again. He does not presume forgiveness as his son. He dares not ask for a second inheritance.

How different this is from my own approach, expecting full restoration by the completion of some meager penance, rattled off my lips in a few minutes. The prodigal son was not only lavish in his spending but lavish in his repentance.

Was his true prodigality in his humility? Is that what I am to learn about meekness and humility in this tale of Yours?

The etymology of prodigal is worth considering. The prefix *pro* (meaning "Forth") and the verb "*agree* (meaning "to drive") shows how the son was driven forth by humility to the feet of his father. He was prodigal in his humility, just as the father was prodigal in his mercy.

The prodigal son, O Lord, reminds me of the good angels that remained with Your Father during the great rebellion. They agreed to serve in whatever capacity the Father so desired, even if this meant bowing before flesh and blood. Meanwhile, Lucifer and his followers proudly proclaimed, and still do from the depths of hell, "*Non serviam*!"

Here, the son does not dream of returning to his father's home as anything other than a hired servant, content with food and drink as payment for service. It is remarkable to see this young man, once accustomed to luxury, not only willing but happy to work as a servant. He cares not of the whispers of the household. There's no pride left within him; it was stamped out in the pig trough. He is untroubled about friends and family seeing him serve at table where he was once served. He was ready and willing to hear the giggles from the girls who once danced with him, now directing him to fill their cups with wine so they can dance more freely with others. He was prepared to labor for his master after the family goes to sleep, to arise before they wake, and sleep a mere few hours in the spartan servants' quarters. He was humble enough to be seen as a servant, fed and clothed as a servant, to sleep like a servant, to work like a servant, to be instructed like a servant.

But even more striking, Lord and God, he was humble enough to be seen as a former son, fed and clothed as a former son, to sleep like a former son, to be instructed like a former son.

Serviam,"I will serve" permeates every pore of his broken body. "I will serve" filled every neural pathway of his mind. "I will serve" was the true intention of his heart. And he was filled with joy to serve, for he knew he did not even deserve to serve. He hoped that the love and mercy of his father might extend far enough to lead him to the servants' quarters.

Yes, Lord, it seems you are teaching me that the true humility of this young man was that he never considered, never even dreamed of being restored as a son to his father. His hope, beyond all hope, was that mercy would restore him to the glory of being a mere servant in his father's house.

Have I ever possessed such humility? Has presumption taken root so deep that true repentance has escaped me?

Despite the sad fact that my heart is unaccustomed to genuine repentance, hear my words, O Lord. In Your infinite mercy, allow me to be a servant in Your heavenly kingdom. I deserve not that place of a baptized son, for I have wasted this inheritance countless times. Please Lord, welcome me through the back door of your servants' quarters, so that I may escape the torment that I truly deserve.

XXIX
Turning to Stone *or* The Rich Young Man

(Mark 10:1–29)

Because of the hardness of my heart, O Lord.[83] This is why Moses gave Your chosen people certain laws, including the one permitting a man to "put away his wife"—a concession to our stubborn spirits.[84]

Our hearts, O Lord—my heart—are as unyielding as the stone upon which You inscribed Your commandments. Your justice is the hammer and chisel; Your mercy, the breath that scatters the remnants to the wind. My heart, hardened by pride and her seven daughters—vainglory, ambition, boasting, arrogance, presumption, hypocrisy, and disobedience—stands as a fortress against Your love. From

---

83 See Mark 10:5.

84 Mark 10:5.

the dawn of time, You saw this heart of stone, one that was also angry, ready to fight any and all for my own glory.

My life, Lord Jesus, mirrors this chapter in Mark with uncanny precision. As You died for me in Your infinite love, did You craft this chapter as a reflection of my soul's journey?

Chapter 10 begins with hardened hearts but swiftly turns to those with the softest hearts—the little children, so dear to You and to me, heirs to the Kingdom of Heaven.[85] My own stubborn heart has been softened by these little ones. Through them, we echo Your divine invitation: "Let the little ones come unto Me."

Your infinite wisdom, Your grand design from creation's first light, placed these passages side by side with purpose. There is no editorial accident here, no arbitrary stroke of Mark's pen. You wanted us to see the stark contrast between hardness of heart and childlike faith.

O, what better way to teach us meekness than to bring children to Your knee and proclaim them inheritors of heaven! If anyone should grasp the depth of Your words about children—why we must become like them to enter Your kingdom—surely it is I. It is without doubt due to their meekness and humility of heart.

You make it clear that softness of heart is required for true discipleship, and that the kingdom belongs to the childlike. And then we grow up. We work hard, we educate ourselves, we tame our youthful impulses. We polish up.

---

85 See Mark 10:13–16.

We get jobs. We learn the ways of adulthood, paying bills, mortgages and insurance, how to save and how to spend. We do not steal, kill or lie. We marry, have children, climb career ladders. We keep the Sabbath, we receive the sacraments, follow the precepts of Your Church. We follow the rules of society, marriage, and parenting. We strive to do everything "right."

And then one day, in the quiet of our prayer, as we meditate upon this young man, we find ourselves in his place in the story, running up to You, O Lord. Are You proud of me? See, I follow all the rules. I avoid all the bad things. See? I do all the good things. See?

But in Your eyes—those dark, piercing eyes—a look of love, shrouding a gaze of disappointment. A sorrow in Your face consumes me. Your eyes are fire and ice. My soul, a moment ago, filled with self-adulation, burns and freezes. I cannot look away from Your sorrow, yet I can bear the sight no more. In purgatory, I stand, locked in a prison of uncertainty, of shame and regret and remorse for having even approached You. You still have not spoken to me. Your eyes, those eyes of mercy and justice. The stillness of Your face is torture. Say something. Please. Break this purgatory of silence and stillness. Move. Speak. Save me from the bondage of Your glare. I am melting away. I am turning to stone. Save me, Lord. Save me.

And then You say, "Go, and sell all You have and give it to the poor, and come follow Me."

XXX
Tears Are More Human than Blood
or
The Rising of Lazarus

(John 11)

Why do we cherish this scene from Your life so deeply, O Lord? Why do we find solace in witnessing You weep? Tears from the very eyes of God, welling up and breaking forth, streaming down the holy face—cheeks kissed by the Virgin Mother, kissed by Your betrayer. We are drawn to the sight of Your reddened eyes, to the quiver of Your lips, to the sound of Your heaving breaths.

"Jesus wept."

Your tears of emotion touch us more profoundly than those shed in suffering.

"Jesus wept." The shortest verse in all of Scripture, yet it might as well say, "Jesus was one of us." Those two words, those three syllables, affirm the reality of the Incarnation. It was not a divine performance or a trick of deception. You did not merely act human; You are human, like us in all things but sin, and in that You are actually *more human* than we who have failed at being so. In seeing You weep here, we connect with Your humanity more than when You wept in the garden, at the pillar of Your scourging, or even upon the cross. You embody not only our humanity but our emotions, erupting and overwhelming.

Tears are more human than blood.

Wild beasts may bleed, but they do not weep. They may mourn for their young in their own way, yet no tears fill the eyes of a mother hen when a serpent steals her chick. My goats wailed when their kids were sold, but wailing is not weeping. My dog appeared melancholic when the runt of the litter died, yet her eyes remained dry.

Tears are more human than blood.

Here, I encounter the full glory of Your humanity, the perfect embodiment of these virtues. You truly are one of us. You are even like me.

But why did You weep, Son of Joseph? The answer seems obvious, drawn from the pages of Scripture. Yet there is a profound misunderstanding, at least in popular thought. Most would say You wept at the tomb of Lazarus because You lost a friend, just as we would mourn our own losses. But I believe this is not the cause of Your tears.

You orchestrated this moment from the beginning. Mary and Martha sent You a message saying the one You loved was sick, and You began to reveal Your plan: "This sickness is not unto death, but for the glory of God."[86] You lingered for two days, waiting for Lazarus to die. Then, You made Your intentions clear to Your disciples, saying, "Lazarus is dead. And I am glad, for Your sakes, that I was not there, that You may believe: but let us go to him."[87]

Why have You not yet wept? Your friend is dead. You waited for him to die, not being present at his deathbed.

Four days he had been in the tomb, and still, You have not wept.

I see you, the divine strategist, wondering if you might not have been a tad anxious about Your greatest miracle yet, also reluctant knowing that word of power over death would travel far and wide. You will sacrifice Your life to save Lazarus's. You've set the stage for a spectacle that will not only glorify God but will spread through the land like wildfire, striking the hearts of many in myriad ways.

Martha, the one You gently admonished to focus on one thing rather than many, rushes to meet You. In her limited way, she possesses faith. You tell her that her brother will rise again, and she professes her belief in the resurrection on the last day. You reveal to her that You are that resurrection and the life. She accepts this and sends for her sister Mary. Yet still, You have not wept.

Then Mary arrives, the one who sat at Your feet, free from anxiety, the same who anointed Your feet with pre-

86 John 11:4.

87 John 11:14–15.

cious ointment. Once again, she impresses You with her humility and faith. "When Mary therefore was come where Jesus was, seeing him, she fell down at his feet, and saith to him: Lord, if You had been here, my brother would not have died."[88] And then, the moment of meekness arrives.

"Jesus, therefore, when He saw her weeping, and the Jews who had come with her weeping, groaned in the spirit and troubled Himself."[89] You did not weep at the thought of Your friend's death; You knew You would see him again. You were not moved by the sight of his sealed tomb, for You had not yet reached it. Yet, witnessing the love and compassion of Your friends and the mourners present, You were stirred in spirit. You were moved by their sorrow, by their mourning, by their compassion. Perhaps You were saddened by the consequences of sin in this dark world and the pain it inflicts upon those who love. Perhaps You felt a certain guilt for allowing them to suffer for four days rather than comforting them. Perhaps You were seized by an agony of fear and dread as to the passion that was about to ensue. Whatever the cause, Your spirit groaned.

You asked where Lazarus was laid. They replied, "Come and see." And then, the moment came.

"Jesus wept."[90]

Perhaps the most beautiful words of Scripture.

---

88 John 11:32.

89 John 11:33.

90 John 11:35.

Whatever the cause of Your tears, You wept. You did not just shed a tear. You wept. Did Your knees buckle? Did You bury Your face in Your hands? It must have been a sight that struck fear and confusion in the hearts of Your disciples.

The next verse puts into words the very misunderstanding we often have about Your tears: "The Jews, therefore, said, 'Behold how He loved him'" (John 11:36). They knew not what we understand. They did not realize that You had orchestrated this moment, that for at least four days You had known of Lazarus's death, that You waited for it, that You had foretold it to Your disciples, and that You proclaimed, "I am glad for Your sakes that I was not there, that You may believe." They could not see that You hold life and death in the very hands that wiped away Your tears, that You are the resurrection and the life. They knew none of this, and thus they assumed Your tears were for Lazarus. But I think not.

Throughout Your Gospel, Lord, You seem moved by the smallest acts of kindness, compassion, and generosity. The widow's mite holds more value than gold. The smallest mustard seed can move mountains; the humility and innocence of children surpass the power of man. The lost sheep holds greater value to the Shepherd than the flock, or the simple kindness of the Good Samaritan reveals the depth of Your compassion.

O Lord, King of Compassion, make our hearts like unto Thine. For those who mourn shall be comforted. What greater meekness can there be?

Tears are more human than blood.

XXXI
The Price of Heaven
or
The Widow's Mite

(Mark 12:41–44; Luke 21:1–4)

O Lord, King of Kings, Son of the humble carpenter, how it must have grieved Your heart to see the clerics of long robes, seeking the first chairs in the synagogues, the highest places of supper.[91] These were the Scribes and Pharisees, the men of God's holy law, who devoured the houses of widows under the pretense of long prayers. Hypocrites, whitewashed tombs.

The law called them to humility, but they were puffed up with pride. Called to gentleness by the love of God, yet they met the lonely, the oppressed, and the poor with exploitation. Service to the least among us could never fill their days, for their hearts were brimming with self-interest.

---

91 See Mark 12:38–39.

True piety should have been a subtle fragrance, a modest offering to the Divine, yet their hypocrisy unfurled like a banner, seeking veneration from all who passed by.

All for the glory of self, not the glory of God.

"These shall receive greater condemnation."[92]

Your followers, Lord God, had an earful about these hypocrites, these vipers. You showed us time and again what not to be. But here, a new emphasis arises.

A certain poor widow entered.[93] In my mind's eye, I see an old woman, hunched over, limping toward the offertory box, strands of unkempt gray hair escaping her veil. How long had her husband been gone? Two months? Two years? Two decades? Were there grown children to care for her? Were there grandchildren to bring her joy?

Or was she a 33-year-old mother with a half-dozen children, some working to help pay the bills, some toddlers in tow? Was her teenager angry she gave the two mites from their limited supply?

A mite, the smallest coin used at that time, was worth no more than half a dollar today.

Who would think much of a dollar? Who would need it? Yet, for the rest of human history, this widow's mite will symbolize a charitable donation given from the heart, more valuable than vast treasures donated for the sake of pride.

What is my widow's mite, O Lord? Do I give You the dollar she gave, which was from her necessity, or do I give

---

92 Mark 12:40.

93 See Mark 12:42.

you a dollar from the overflowing edges of my surplus? Do I love You with all my treasure or with my extra change? The Divine King needs not my treasure, but desperately desires His own treasure. And my soul, this little and wretched, yet eternal, soul made in Your image, is Your treasure. I came from You, and You want me back. I am Yours. I am a widow's mere mite. But I am Yours.

You, Divine Master, meek and humble of heart, draw our eyes to a mite. The meekness of the mite holds the power to purchase the Kingdom of Heaven, just as the faith of a mustard seed can move mountains. Your inheritance, O Lord, is on sale. It can be purchased by no vast fortune, but only a mite given in meekness and humility. A little mite, worth more than all the riches in all the kingdoms of this world.

XXXII
Atop Your Warhorse
or
Entry into Jerusalem

(Matthew 21:1–11; Mark 11:1–10;
Luke 19:28–40; John 12:12–19)

Upon a warhorse You ride, resplendent in garments of purest white, ablaze with the brilliance of a thousand suns. The ground quakes beneath Your steed's mighty hooves, treading upon a royal carpet woven from the finest cloaks of Your zealous legionaries and their palm branches of victory and peace, strewn together in devotion. This divine moment, O Lord, foretelling what was pre-ordained from all eternity.

Your twelve battle-hardened guardians, soon to protect not Your person but Your holy mission, stand steadfast in solidarity. Unwavering zeal and readiness, prepare to give their all, willing to be the last standing.

The spirit is willing.

They will never abandon You, deny You, betray You—not for half of Herod's kingdom.

Bold and brilliant, You enter the enemy's camp with Your loyal retinue, ready to receive Your crown adorned with precious crimson jewels. You will be lifted high above the place of skulls for all to witness Your splendor and sovereignty, conquering the darkness of this world, arms outstretched to welcome all into the kingdom You have reclaimed.

This, my divine King, is the true essence of Your entry into Jerusalem. Yet, in Your boundless humility and meekness, this majestic truth is veiled as You ride a donkey, surrounded by the poor and oppressed, their humble garments scattered on the dusty path. Your devoted followers lead You into the heart of suffering, only to fall asleep, to flee, to hide, to sell You for thirty pieces of silver, and to deny even knowing You.

The scourging awaits You, a crown of thorns, mockery, and death. The march to Calvary, the nails piercing Your hands and feet, death by excruciating agony. Yet we see only the suffering because You are meek and humble of heart. The true glory remains hidden for all to see on another day.

O Lord, make my heart like unto Thine.

XXXIII
Into Your Hands
or
The Last Supper

(Matthew 26:17–30; Mark 14:12–26;
Luke 22:7–23; John 13:1–30)

O, most Holy Eucharist, O Sacrament Divine.

In Your infinite wisdom and meekness, You place Yourself at the call of sinful humanity, granting Your priests the power to summon You from heaven's throne into the dark corners of our fallen world. On that sacred eve of Your great sacrifice, You gave us Your greatest sacrament.

In that quiet upper room, You, the King of Kings, knelt before a rabble of sinful men, washing their dirty feet, turning upside down all notions of mastery and service: the last shall be first, the first shall be last, the greatest among you will become the least. Did Your followers understand? Did they have to wait for the grace of the Spirit to enlighten their dense minds?

As the evening deepened, Your submission to the Father's will continued evermore. You took bread in Your sacred and venerable hands, blessed and broke it. You lifted the cup, sealing a new and everlasting covenant. By Your humility, You made permanent the ability of any priest to call You from paradise, offering You as the bloodless victim to the Father. The notion of dying a thousand deaths for a loved one was consummated upon the altar of that upper room.

You become food and drink for hungry souls. You allow Yourself to be imprisoned in tabernacles as we busy ourselves seeking worldly solace. Your presence is available always, everywhere. Saints implore us to visit You. Your presence heralded only by a faint, flickering light.

Confined within that silent tabernacle, You wait patiently, that little red candlelight inviting us to a sacred pause, to enjoy a moment of peace amidst an anxious world. In a moment of half-baked piety, we try to fit You into our schedules.

In the face of the world's doubt and mockery, You remain still and silent and present, teaching us the power of meekness. You could reveal Your might through grand spectacle, mesmerizing all the world in any and every church across the globe, yet You choose to remain silent as You did before the powers of this world—Caiaphas, Herod, Pilate. Like a lamb before its shearer, You embody humility and meekness.

Back on that sorrowful night, You watched Your betrayer share Your bowl, knowing his plan, yet ordaining him a bishop, foreshadowing future betrayals within Your sacred priesthood.

You humbly allow the unworthy to call You down, but also the unworthy to consume You. As You were led to Calvary, You are led to the corrupt abodes of our sinful bodies.

While You suffer the injustice of being devoured, we balk at the slightest act of being disrespected. We endure nearly nothing from those who approach us with injustice, while You surrender Yourself to all who approach Your altar.

On the holy cross You proclaimed, "Into Your hands, O Lord, I commend my spirit," entrusting Yourself wholly to the Father. In the Eucharist, You commend Yourself into our hands, Your body, blood, soul, and divinity.

Every time I have approached Your altar, You have commended Yourself to me. Will I commend myself to You?

XXXIV
Widen the Vessel of Suffering
or
Agony in the Garden

(Matthew 26:36–46; Mark 14:32–42; Luke 22:39–46)

No greater act of humility, none, than this: to breathe and believe, "Not my will, but Thine be done."[94] How often, O Lord of sorrows, have I murmured this sacred phrase. How seldom have I meant it.

Your agony—agony. What a word! Is there a more fitting term? How else can the human tongue twist to tell the depth of Your scourging, crowning, crucifixion? What other word captures the torment You bore, seeing my sins, despite Your boundless gifts and grace, my cushioned life, my nurturing and support? How can I, who ponders Your agony, still sin? How? I hold the power to lessen Your suffering by sinning less, for even my slightest

[94] Luke 22:42.

transgression is stacked upon Your immeasurable agony in the garden.

You "grew sorrowful." The vision of Your impending passion swelled within Your mind's eye. You sought the faintest comfort from Your Peter, James, and John, and confided, "My soul is sorrowful even unto death."[95]

And unto death You came, Your humanity unable to bear the weight. You pleaded with Your Father, "If Thou wilt, remove this chalice from me."[96] You broke.

It seems the angel did not come to comfort You as much to "strengthen" You, enabling You to persist in Your prayerful agony.[97] The angel's touch allowed You to transcend human limitations, so that You could humbly endure all the sins of the world.

Truly, O Lord, human nature, when infused with divine grace, is capable of anything save for two acts reserved for divinity: create out of nothing and annihilate into nothing.

But all else—giving sight to the blind, making the lame walk, the deaf hear, raising the dead, conquering sin, redeeming mankind—all can be accomplished through human nature. And here, on the Mount of Olives, You pushed the bounds of human nature. The angel strengthened You so that Your humanity could expand to bear the pain of all sins ever committed, more striking and terrifying than a thousand bombs set off within a single body, held together

95 Matt. 26:37–38.

96 Luke 22:42.

97 See Luke 22:43.

by the grace of God. There was no limit to the pain You could have felt. So much so that You begged Your Abba three times to let this cup pass.[98]

But no.

Rather, He commanded the angel to increase the bounds of Your endurance, to widen the vessel of Your suffering, to stretch the sinews of Your fortitude, to deepen the well of Your meekness as the horizon of Your agony expanded on and on through the night.

Ah, the humility to endure until Your Father decreed otherwise, until the price for our sins, my sins, had been fully paid! The angel increased Your threshold, and it was filled to the point of bursting, blood erupting from Your pores, spilling to the ground, consecrating this mortal coil like the drops of water on a babe's head at baptism.

Never before had such suffering been endured. Never again will it be endured. It was one for all the ages, one for eternity.

Do we ask for our threshold for suffering to expand? Do we beseech our angels to strengthen rather than comfort us?

I see now that humility is the willingness to ever increase our suffering in order to unite with You, who paid the price for our sins. My Lord and my God, make my heart like unto Thine.

---

[98] See Matt. 26:39–44.

XXXV
Dumb as a Lamb
or
The Trial

(Matthew 26:57–27:15)

"He was offered because it was his own will, and he opened not his mouth: he shall be led as a sheep to the slaughter, and shall be dumb as a lamb before his shearer, and he shall not open his mouth."[99]

Upon Your betrayer's kiss in the garden, Your trial began. How exhausted You must have been from the agony already endured, blood still dripping from Your pores like sacred dew. The Sanhedrin's temple guards, their torches casting light upon Your flesh, could not discern from which wound Your blood flowed. Yet the severing of Malchus's ear diverted their gaze, and the new blood that flowed distracted them. They saw the miraculous healing, yet carried out

[99] Is. 53:7.

their orders and led You to Your trial. Did this miracle strike doubt into their hearts? One would think. Yet still, You, the Prince of Peace, were led like a lamb to the slaughter.

Did You, O Lord, think of Isaiah's prophecy on Your way? Did You whisper to Your own heart, "Hold Your tongue, hold Your tongue"? Was it a conscious act to fulfill the prophecy, or were You just being Yourself?

Days before, the streets were alive with song and praise, palm branches and cloaks laid down as a royal carpet for Your procession. Now, those same people, safe in their homes, peeked through shutters to witness the raucous parade in the streets. Whispers spread like a virus through Your mystical body, infecting them with doubt, branding You a fraud, a false prophet, an imposter, and perhaps murmuring little prayers of repentance for hailing You as their Messiah. What suffering You endured to be seen no longer as a savior, but a common criminal in chains.

You, the Pascal Lamb, stood before the bloodthirsty Caiaphas, who sought false witnesses against You.[100] He challenged You, offering a chance to defend Yourself.

I recall the revelation to Saint Anselm, where Your Blessed Mother, confident in Your eloquence, believed in Your ability to defend and explain Yourself. "But Jesus held his peace," in humility and meekness.[101] Your silence was yet another sword piercing her heart.

---

100 See Matt. 26:59–60.

101 St. Anselm of Canterbury, *The Passion of Christ Through the Eyes of Mary* (TAN Books, 2022), 16–18.

When questioned, You simply replied, "Thou hast said *it*. Nevertheless, I say to You, hereafter you shall see the Son of Man sitting on the right hand of the power of God, and coming in the clouds of heaven."[102]

Here, O Lord, before this high priest, this false pontiff of reverence and piety, You had the chance to perform one more miracle. You could have set the record straight, compelled all to bow before You. Like Elijah, You could have called fire down from heaven[103] or like Moses made water spring from the stone upon which You stood.[104] Like Joshua You could have commanded the moon that glistened down upon you to stand still[105] or called thunder and rain from the sky as Samuel did.[106] With any such miracle, You could have taken Your seat upon Caiaphas's throne, leaving no doubt to Your claims.

It would have required but a slight display of power, effortless for You. Your disciples would have returned, Your mother seated at Your right hand, and Caiaphas would have either accepted You or been thrown out.

Or perhaps not. Perhaps the hardness of heart beneath those ceremonial robes was impenetrable. Could You have raised a thousand prophets from the dead before their eyes, and still they would have executed You? Was their pride

---

102 Matt. 26:64.

103 See 1 Kgs. 18.

104 See Ex. 17:6.

105 See Jos. 10:12–24.

106 See 1 Kgs. 12:16–18.

insurmountable? Were their hearts closed even to the most evident signs of Your divinity?

Why, O Lord, did You fill the last three years with marvels of divine proportion, capturing the faith of the poor and downtrodden, opening their eyes, lifting the lame, multiplying loaves and fishes, walking on water, raising the dead, and when the moment came to claim Your throne, to rally the power of Judaism, You did nothing? Even worse than nothing, You emboldened them, likening Yourself to the Son of Man sitting at the right hand of God in the clouds of heaven without any evidence to back it up. What happened?

And You stood silent—silent as a lamb before its shearer.

Peter watched from afar. He must have asked the same question. "Why don't You prove Yourself? Justify Yourself. Justify me! Why do You stand there like a dumb lamb?"

And then the abuse began.

They spat in Your most holy face, vile saliva and foul mucus cast upon Your eyes, cheeks, and lips. How many men lined up, one after another?

And then they struck You, one after another. Did their fists wound more deeply than their mockery? "Prophesy unto us, O Christ, who is he that struck thee?"[107] After covering You in spit and mucus, did they also cover Your head, taunting You to identify Your abuser? These were men of God, well-versed in the Torah, filled with Your Father's law of love and compassion. Men of the cloth, awaiting the

---

107 Matt. 26:68.

Messiah, should have known the ways of God—meekness, humility, mercy, and peace. How did their minds overlook all of this? How did they twist Scripture to justify cruelty and mockery?

Did You make eye contact with Peter? With Your mother? With any of Your friends?

And then, off to the dungeon for the night before being taken to Pilate.

I have read of the pit where You spent that night, torturous in itself, not much larger than Your hunched-over body. The pain, the darkness, the loneliness, the fear of the chalice You would drink upon the rising sun.

I think of the strength required to endure this trial, the patience required to be chained in a pit, awaiting Your fate. Did You think to Yourself, "Let's get this over with"? Did You cherish every moment left on this earth, to pray to Your Father, to suffer just a little more for humanity?

How little am I able to endure mockery! How quickly I fight back, defend my name, justify my actions. How often I have been unwilling to allow any mistaken belief of my thoughts, actions, or disposition go uncorrected. I will use any and all power I have to right the wrongs done to me. I will not be spit upon. I will not be mocked. I will certainly not be struck.

I, silly little man, have no power but am filled with pride; You have infinite power and are filled with humility.

The morning came. You were bound and brought to Pilate. Again, did Isaiah come to mind? Did You tell Yourself,

"Hold Your tongue"? Did You plan to be as silent as a lamb, or was it simply Your nature?

Then, O Lord, You were taken to King Herod, whose father sought Your life while You were but a child. To him, You spoke not a word. At least to Caiaphas and Pilate You uttered a few words. But to Herod, You remained utterly silent. "And he questioned him in many words. But He answered him nothing."[108] True, Your meekness is obvious as You patiently and silently stand accused. But I see Your silence as a turning away from those of this world, a withdrawal of grace, a shunning. I would rather be those who You reprimand than those You ignore.

How mighty and terrible is Your silence. I beg You, O Lord, to never be silent to me. Let me hear anything other than Your silence. It will deafen me. It will crush me. And I will be lost forever.

---

[108] Luke 23:9.

XXXVI
The Lamb Before Its Shearer
or
The Scourging

(Matthew 27:26; John 19:1)

You not only took the form of a slave, says Your great servant Saint Bernard of Clairvaux, but You took the form of a bad slave, the slave of sin, deserving the lash and to suffer the harshest punishment.

Yet, a hidden truth emerges from this scene of You chained to the pillar. Layers upon layers of meaning unfold as I read this famous passage through the lens of meekness and humility.

How many times my eyes drifted past Your scouring, blind to the reality of my own chains, a prisoner of sin with the rest of humanity, deserving the flagellum myself time and time again. The powers of hell, those legions of darkness, lure us like sirens. They ensnarl us in their grasp, desirous of nothing less than tormenting us eternally, taking out their hatred of humanity—of You—on us.

They despise humanity, for it was flesh they refused to adore at the Incarnation. They will forever resent skin, blood, muscle, and bone, which they perceive as the cause of their downfall. So many people think demons love the flesh, but in fact they hate it with a passion beyond our powers. And thus, they lead us into sins of the flesh, pointing out to one another the grotesqueness, rejoicing in our downfall. Each sin of the flesh is a slight toward the Incarnation itself. And the demons know it.

But did they know who You really were? We do not know. Tradition holds they were aware of a pending incarnation, perhaps the very cause of their flight from heaven. But tradition also holds that Your true presence was hidden from them during Your earthly life. In any event, they certainly knew You were a man with power over them, a man whom they could never conquer even with the slightest venial sin.

I envision, Lord God, demons fighting with anxious zeal to possess the Romans wielding the flagellum: one chance in eternity to scourge this mysterious man of God, perhaps he who the prophets proclaimed, perhaps more. Did Lucifer grant favor to his chosen children? Did he bestow the right to Beelzebub for his pride and gluttony, or Moloch for his thirst for sacrificial children,[109] or Abaddon as a prefigurement of the torment he will unleash on the last

---

109 See Lev. 18:21.

day?[110] Or did he appease many by granting Legion their turn?

They forfeited paradise, refusing to bow before your flesh, and now, Your flesh was brought to its knees before them, chained to a pillar, exposed by the rending of Your garments. Your flesh exposed and vulnerable. They, like a pack of ravenous dogs before a dying animal circle, fangs sharp with insatiable bloodlust. A chilling cacophony of growls sending shivers down my spine.

Your back, bare and meek, awaits the price for my sin, the metal-tipped leather straps tearing into Your sacred flesh, casting it across the Praetorium. Mystics, granted visions of Your scourging, speak of flesh torn so deeply that ribs lay bare. My mind considers how life emerged from the old Adam's rib, as your Father, with surgical precision, opened his side to create the mother of us all, who would usher sin into the world, casting us into bondage.

Yet You, the new Adam, freely allow the darkness to expose Your rib, from which sacred blood flows to sanctify me, Your unworthy servant. Your scourging, Lord, a death sentence to many, embodies a meekness and humility impossible for one to grasp.

You were, indeed, led like a lamb to the slaughter, not to shed wool but to sever flesh, the sacrificial lamb in countless ways.

---

110 See St. John Apoc. 9:11.

XXXVII
Mockery of Your Father's Kingdom
or
The Crowning of Thorns

(Matthew 27:29–30; Mark 15:17–19)

My Lord Jesus, King of Kings, my mind fixates on the mockery of Your crown of thorns more than on the excruciating pain of their being crushed into Your sacred head, pressed down by a reed, nerves exploding in agony, ringing out louder than cathedral bells.

This crown tormented You until the end, delivering fresh gashes into Your scalp with every movement as You hung upon the cross. Even in exhaustion, You could find no rest for Your head.

Despite this agony, despite the obvious imagery of each thorn representing my sins piercing Your precious brow, I remain transfixed by the mockery itself.

You were mocked as King of the Jews, dressed in purple, given a reed as a scepter, Your tormentors bowing in cruel jest, striking and spitting upon You. But what was the most painful part of this, O Lord?

If anger welled within You, I imagine it was in defense of Your Father's kingdom. You who twice drove the money changers from the temple in righteous fury—did that same wrath not threaten to burst forth now? You let Your anger show for Your Father's honor then, would not the same anger for Your Father's honor show now? You let your anger show for Your Father's temple made of stone, but not for His temple made of flesh and bone?

I think, my God, the anger boiled like molten lava, threatening to burst from the surface, consuming all around in a single apocalyptic moment of terror and retribution. Yet here You teach us again to be meek and humble of heart. Your Father's plan was at hand. The cup had not passed from You. Strengthened by an angel, You became the Lamb ready for slaughter.

You endured not just mockery of Yourself, but of Your Father's kingdom.

There You sat, stripped of flesh and dignity, accepting the taunts and insults of Your subjects, just as a king would hear the praises and pleas of his people. You are the King of Tears, the King of Suffering, the King of Passion, inviting me to glory in Your cross, inviting me to embrace my own. Can I too wear this crown of meekness and humility, or is my head too big? Does it interrupt my ideas? Does it mess up my hair? Is it embarrassing to wear such a crown? Can my meekness endure the mockery of men? Or will I cast off that crown of pain and humiliation and fight back with the same wrath that placed the crown on Your head to begin with?

XXXVIII
The Father Speaks
or
Ecce Homo

(John 19:5)

The following is addressed to God the Father

Heavenly Father, I pen this passage to You with a trembling hand, an unworthy soul, and a heart laden with fear. How effortless it is for me to address Your Son, guided by Your providence in the Incarnation.

Yet, I must speak to You here, for You have spoken to me here.

I marvel at how You, the Master Weaver, the First Cause, the Divine Strategist, employ the most heinous and vicious acts of humanity to unveil Your truth, as if the darkest moments are the very canvas upon which Your light shines most brilliantly.

All things, both good and ill, are vessels of Your boundless love for me, akin to a ship laden with treasures of gold and jewels, hijacked by villainous pirates, yet miraculously delivered unto me. Regardless of the evil one's actions, Your Word will be spoken to me.

Here, on Pilate's balcony, Your Son—so meek and humble of heart—stands for all to behold, presented as a Spouse of Blood, just as He was presented to You thirty-three years prior in the Temple, following the rite of circumcision that sealed His covenant with You.

Jesus stands before me. He has been scourged and crowned with thorns. He has been struck and mocked, enduring it all as gentle as a lamb led to the slaughter.

And here, before the final sacrifice upon the cross, You, Eternal Father, hold Your Son high before me, crowned, wrapped in a purple garment of royalty, as You use Pilate's words, *Ecce homo*, to speak directly to my heart:

> *Behold the Man. Behold Him with whom I am well pleased.*
>
> *Behold Him who will take away the sins of the world.*
>
> *Behold Him, who is meek and humble of heart.*
>
> *All that you aspire to be is present here. All your happiness resides here. The answer to your problems stands before you. No more searching is needed. Behold, here lies the answer to every question, to every dilemma.*
>
> *Behold, here is the Way, the Truth, the Life. Here is your remedy for every sorrow. Here is your peace, your joy.*

Behold, here is the sacrifice that I offer for You. I sacrificed My Son so that you can be My son.

Behold the Man, who stands ready to ascend the altar of Calvary as the spotless Lamb.

Behold, meekness itself.

Behold, humility itself.

Ecce Homo.

Ecce Homo.

Ecce Homo.

XXXIX
Cradle Your Cross
or
You Carry Your Cross

(Matthew 27:31–32; Mark 15:20–21; Luke 23:26; John 19:17)

You were a lamb already slaughtered before ever reaching the altar, O Lord. Your anguish in Gethsemane brought You to death's threshold, until the angel expanded Your capacity for suffering beyond the bounds of mortal endurance. The scourging was executed as a death sentence by bloodlust of demonic proportions.

Now You face a third death sentence. You must bear Your own altar of sacrifice, Your own gibbet upon which to be raised high, a spectacle of deterrence. Half a mile You must meekly endure before spreading out Your body, opening Your hands, and laying flat Your feet to receive their cruel nails.

Yet in this moment, before Your death march begins, Your own prophecy finds fulfillment: "Take up your cross and follow Me."

O Lord, how flippantly I utter these words, applying them to life's smallest irritation: nasty tones of voices, difficult personalities, chores around the house, the little decisions to be made. Shame washes over me as I relate this instrument of torture to my trivial sufferings.

If a real cross appeared in my life, literal or metaphorical, would I run for my life? Would I flee like Peter, denying any association with You?

In my mind's eye, I see You not merely receiving the fifteen-foot beam upon Your shoulders. No. I see you gaze upon the tree of life. I see You reach out for it. I see you grab it, embrace it, invoking more laughter from Your tormentors. There You kneel, cradling Your cross, defying earthly comprehension.

Here I see the deepest levels of humility. You not only endure, but You embrace Your Father's will. My own virtue barely musters the strength to endure the shortest distance. But You cradle Your cross.

I'm not sure that I have ever reached out for a cross, but my mind does comprehend that this is the only place for complete happiness, transcending any bodily comfort available in this life. Though my mind grasps this truth, my soul lacks the strength—or rather, the humility—to set aside longings for comfort and rest and praise and pleasure.

My eyes only see and my ears only hear what my brain is looking for. I look not for the crosses You have given me. But if I did, if I only possessed the humility to cherish Your Father's will above my own, then my eyes and ears would open anew, revealing the crosses lovingly bestowed upon me. They would no longer look so heinous, but shimmer with divine light. And I would cradle them tightly, ever seeking to touch the love concealed in their wooden grain.

XL
Please, Learn of Me *or* The Crucifixion

(Matthew 27:35–37; Mark 15:24–26;
Luke 23:33–34; John 19:18–22)

O Great High Priest, You have borne Your own altar to the Place of Skulls. The meekest of lambs, You lay upon it without guile, resentment, or anger.

The hour of sacrifice has come.

No need for Roman hands to seize You; willingly You stretch forth Your limbs, reaching out for where nails shall pass.

The first pierces flesh, bone, and nerve, sending a hymn of agony heavenward to Your Father. Yet the second piercing eludes Your reach. As mystics recount, ropes stretch Your arm beyond nature's bounds so that the second nail might find its mark. Another sacred song of suffering ascends.

These hands, that once bestowed sight to the blind, that healed countless sick and lame, that touched the untouchable leper, that consecrated the first Eucharist mere hours ago, now lie fixed to Your bed of pain, Your throne of love.

The hammer's echo resounds through the mountains, reaching the ears of Your mother Mary, who has accompanied You in Your death march. O, these sacred hands, now paying redemption's price for every sin of touch, in anger and in lust.

Again and again, the hammer falls, driving nails through the thick bones, muscles, tendons, and nerves of Your holy feet. These feet of the Good Shepherd in search of the last lost sheep, that trod the desert for forty days, that walked upon water, that were anointed with tears and dried with hair. A symphony of agony sung to Your Father. While we use our feet in pursuit of pleasure, comfort, wealth, power, Your feet have paid the price for every selfish step we've taken.

The cross drops hard into its earthen socket, jolting Your wounds against the nails, stretching the gaping holes.

You hang between two thieves, a great thief Yourself who stole souls from Satan's grasp. Steal me too, O Lord, I pray.

Your life, Great Priest, has been a school of perfection for all Your students. "Learn from Me, for I am meek and humble of heart." Every action of Your thirty-three years has been a lesson in these virtues, which this unworthy book has tried to convey.

Here, in Your final hours, You have carried not only Your altar to Calvary but Your pulpit to deliver Your greatest sermon yet.

Yes, my Great Preacher, Your most profound discourse was not on that other mount where You gave us the Beatitudes and the discourse on the Breath of Life. No, it was on this mount of skulls and death. You bore Your pulpit to its apex, ascending so that all might witness the greatest sermon ever delivered in this world.

Here, You gave us a sermon on meekness, humility, and love. Few words were needed, for Your actions spoke volumes. It is as if with each labored breath You beg me to look and learn. As if You say:

> *"Please, learn of Me, learn of Me!*
> *See what it means to be meek.*
> *See what it means to be humble.*
> *See what it means to love."*

Now I see, Lord Jesus, Your words "Learn of Me" have led me to the foot of Your bloody pulpit. And You plead with me, implore me with Your dying breath, to learn, learn, learn.

"Learn from Me. Don't stop watching, please. Don't stop listening to My agony of love. My final and greatest sermon was crafted just for you. All I have taught you through parables and lessons is here, hanging on this cross. This is what it means to love. Are you seeing? Are you hearing? Do you understand?"

"Please, my beloved, learn of Me, for I am meek and humble of heart."

Image Credits

Illustrations by Gustav Doré are in the public domain via Internet Archive.

Illustrations by Albrech Durer, on pages 20 and 30, are in the public domain via the Met Museum.

Page 100: *The Leper* by Alexandre Bida (lithograph) © Look and Learn / Bridgeman Images.

Page 106: *Healing of the Centurian's Servant* by Alexandre Bida (engraving) © Look and Learn / Bridgeman Images.

Page 118: *The Calling of Matthew* by Alexandre Bida (lithograph) © Look and Learn / Bridgeman Images.

Page 162: *The Rich Young Man* by Albert Robida (engraving) © Look and Learn / Bridgeman Images.

Page 188: *Jesus Before Pilate* by Albert Robida (engraving) © Look and Learn / Bridgeman Images.